The High-heeled Leader

*Embrace your feminine power
in life and work*

Katie Day

BALBOA.
PRESS

A DIVISION OF HAY HOUSE

Balboa Press books may be ordered through booksellers or by contacting:

Balboa Press
A Division of Hay House
1663 Liberty Drive
Bloomington, IN 47403
www.balboapress.com
1-(877) 407-4847

Because of the dynamic nature of the Internet, any web addresses or links contained in this book may have changed since publication and may no longer be valid. The views expressed in this work are solely those of the author and do not necessarily reflect the views of the publisher, and the publisher hereby disclaims any responsibility for them.

The author of this book does not dispense medical advice or prescribe the use of any technique as a form of treatment for physical, emotional, or medical problems without the advice of a physician, either directly or indirectly. The intent of the author is only to offer information of a general nature to help you in your quest for emotional and spiritual well-being. In the event you use any of the information in this book for yourself, which is your constitutional right, the author and the publisher assume no responsibility for your actions.

Certain stock imagery © Thinkstock.
Any people depicted in stock imagery provided by Thinkstock are models, and such images are being used for illustrative purposes only.

ISBN: 978-1-4525-5125-8 (e)
ISBN: 978-1-4525-5126-5 (sc)
ISBN: 978-1-4525-5127-2 (hc)

Library of Congress Control Number: 2012908457

Printed in the United States of America

Balboa Press rev. date: 6/18/2012

This book is for every strong, fabulous, talented,
amazing, beautiful, courageous
and magnificent woman out there –
past, present and future.

But most of all, this book is for

YOU.

Because you ARE strong, fabulous, talented,
amazing, beautiful, courageous and
magnificent.

To Marsha

hope you enjoy it

CONTENTS

Imagine a Woman
Patricia Lynn Reilly

Imagine a woman who believes it is right and good she is a woman.
A woman who honors her experience and tells her stories.
Who refuses to carry the sins of others within her body and life.

Imagine a woman who trusts and respects herself.
A woman who listens to her needs and desires.
Who meets them with tenderness and grace.

Imagine a woman who acknowledges the past's influence on the present.
A woman who has walked through her past.
Who has healed into the present.

Imagine a woman who authors her own life.
A woman who exerts, initiates, and moves on her own behalf.
Who refuses to surrender except to her truest self and wisest voice.

Imagine a woman who names her own gods.
A woman who imagines the divine in her image and likeness.
Who designs a personal spirituality to inform her daily life.

Imagine a woman in love with her own body.
A woman who believes her body is enough, just as it is.
Who celebrates its rhythms and cycles as an exquisite resource.

Imagine a woman who honors the body of the Goddess in
her changing body.
A woman who celebrates the accumulation of her years and her wisdom.
Who refuses to use her life-energy disguising the changes in
her body and life.

Imagine a woman who values the women in her life.
A woman who sits in circles of women.
Who is reminded of the truth about herself when she forgets.

Imagine yourself as this woman.

'Women still have an uneasy relationship with power and the traits necessary to be a leader. There is this internalised fear that if we are really powerful, we are going to be considered ruthless or pushy or strident – all those epithets that strike right at our femininity. We are still working at trying to overcome the fear that power and womanliness are mutually exclusive.'

Arianna Huffington, *Newsweek*, October 2007

Foreword

I first met Katie when we were invited to speak at the same conference. She impressed me immediately as someone who was passionate, inspirational and a skilled speaker, who 'walks her talk' as a true high-heeled leader in an honest and uplifting way.

Katie's book reflects her voice. She writes from the heart as well as personal experience. *The High-heeled Leader* is a call for women to be true to themselves and to take responsibility for their own opportunities, successes and setbacks. She empowers women by encouraging them to make the best of themselves – through the way they look, dress and communicate with others – and importantly, through the way they think.

All too often self-limiting thoughts and behaviour can restrict the potential for success. Katie's book will help you to see that you can do anything you put your mind to – by programming your thoughts and therefore your words and your deeds – for success. She explores the importance of being clear about your personal values and provides a practical workbook to encourage women to get out of their own way and discover the value of being proud of their own accomplishments.

Women create their own brand, and therefore their success, from the inside out. Your outer image has an impact on the way you feel about yourself and how others respond to you. In order to become successful in business it is important to have a strong relationship with yourself and to have belief in your goals and what you can achieve. But in order to have a good relationship with others, we first need to have a strong relationship with ourselves. Who better to advise women on how to achieve this than Katie Day.

Bev James, best-selling author of *Do It! or Ditch It*
CEO The Entrepreneurs' Business Academy, January 2012

The High-heeled Leader

Introduction
How To Use This Book

'If you judge people, you have no time to love them.'
Mother Theresa

Firstly – welcome! It's fabulous to have you here and onboard. And thank you for buying my book! I really hope that wherever you are in your life right now, you get something from the following pages and you feel empowered to step into your true power and glory and SHINE.

This is OUR TIME. The time for women to truly embrace their feminine power and energy and celebrate the very essence of who we are. Remembering to celebrate the men in the world at the same time, for the gifts they give too.

The twenty first century and beyond is about collaboration and unity, not the 'them and us' scenario and mind set that have prevailed in the past. We are all unique and magnificent, whatever our gender, age, social or economic situation, what I want is for you to honour YOU – in every way and every day.

The book is in five parts :

Setting The Scene • Who Are You On The Outside?
Who Are You On The Inside? • Using This In The Real World
Time For Celebration

Throughout the book there are various exercises and opportunities for you to set actions for yourself. Please don't feel obliged to follow the book page by page, exercise by exercise. This is your book – it's up to you how you use it.

You may find it really helpful to start at the beginning and finish at the end. However, you may find it more helpful to dip in and out as the mood, and your intuition, takes you. You may want to go back to the exercises and complete them when it feels right to do so.

I would suggest photocopying the exercises before you start, in case you want to complete them more than once – for instance, going back to them six or twelve months later to see if you have changed.

I also want to give you permission to write in this book. Make as much mess and scribble as much as you want to, use coloured pens, doodle in the margins, whatever takes your fancy.

Part One is a bit about me, setting the scene and establishing my credibility with you as the reader as to why you should continue reading. I have written this chapter so you can see where I've come from and to give you an example of some of my life experiences. I have been on this journey and I'm not asking you to do anything that I haven't done myself. I know how challenging it was for me at times, so I want to assure you that I do understand if you come up against your own blocks, but I also know that when I pushed through my own walls and found the light awaiting me on the other side, the struggle was worth it.

Part Two is the start of your personal exploration. 'Who Are You On The Outside' is about you getting in touch with your outer beauty and accepting that wherever you are in your life in terms of age, experience, accomplishments or self-belief, you are gorgeous in your own, unique way. Once you have accepted, and taken ownership of, your external beauty, you are much better placed to continue the exploration on the inside.

Part Three is about looking at who you are internally. We look at what you may or may not be doing to get in your own way, examining what you stand for and how you operate in life. We explore any limiting beliefs you may hold and how you might dispel those and move forward with a lighter and clearer mind-set.

Part Four is how you can transfer all this information back into the working world – whether you work for a company as an employee, whether you run your own business, whether you are thinking about running your own business, or you simply want to transfer the skills and lessons learnt into every day life.

Part Five is your story. Going forward, who do you want to be and how are you going to take yourself there. It's an opportunity for you to really celebrate every aspect of YOU and jump for joy!

At the back of the book is a Resources section. A list of some fabulous women and gorgeous places that will help you enhance your wonderfulness and nourish your mind, body and spirit.

The journey isn't necessarily going to be easy. I'll challenge you frequently along the way, and there may be times when you might be tempted to stop. But I would encourage you to keep going and push through. As the light at the end of the tunnel gets brighter and brighter, the pain along the way will fall into insignificance.

I KNOW YOU'RE BRILLIANT, FABULOUS, GORGEOUS
AND TALENTED – ARE YOU READY TO
BELIEVE IT YOURSELF?

Fantastic – let's get started.

Part One
Setting The Scene

Chapter One
My Story

'A woman with a voice is by definition a strong woman. But the search to find that voice can be remarkably difficult.'
Melinda Gates, Woman's Day Magazine, *October 2 2007*

So, why write this book?

I grew up in the 1960s and 1970s when the world was very different to the way it is now.

I can vividly remember a night in 1970, I was ten. My mum and I had left my dad the previous year and initially we stayed with my aunt, but moved around a lot as Mum was desperately trying to find some stability for us both. We were temporarily staying with a girl-friend of hers who wanted Mum to go on holiday with her. Mum said 'no' as any money she could earn she wanted to save to find us somewhere to live. Mum's friend became really angry and threw us out of her house. It was ten o'clock on a Thursday night, I had to go to school the next day, and we were walking the streets of Bromley with a suitcase and a couple of carrier bags and nowhere to sleep that night.

Mum tried really hard to get us somewhere to stay, all the time trying to make it a huge adventure for me so I wouldn't be scared. A lot of the B&Bs or Guest Houses wouldn't take us in, at that time a woman on her own with a child was viewed as highly suspicious and people didn't want to get involved. Eventually she did find us a room in a B&B to stay that night. We were there for three nights before she managed to find a single room in a large house, we had no beds, just two mattresses on the floor, no fridge or cooker, just a two-ring gas hob. The bathroom we shared with everyone else in the house, all men. All our belongings were in bags in the corner of the room. We were there for about six months in total until mum was able to find us somewhere else to live. We had already had quite a few adventures over the previous eighteen months since we had left Dad with the places we had lived, too much to go into here. The place we ended up in was the top half of a semi-detached house, we had one bedroom, a sitting room and a tiny kitchen. We shared the bathroom with the owner of the house, a very old lady who lived downstairs. She used to come up stairs every morning with an overfull chamber pot which she emptied in the shared bathroom. So my job before I left for school was cleaning the bathroom floor, with mum doing her best with the stair carpet. We were there until mum met my step-dad when I was fourteen and, for the first time since I was nine, we had a whole flat for the three of us, and I had my own bedroom.

Why am I telling you this? Because the strength of character, determination and fight that mum had to draw on to get us through those five years before she met my step-dad was immense. Combine this with her strength to leave my dad in the first place. Even though she knew it was the right thing to do for both of us, back in 1969 it wasn't a decision a woman made without a lot of soul searching. Mum didn't work, so had no independent financial stability and had to rely completely on her estranged husband for support, which she didn't get. This was also the time before the Child Support Agency existed. Mum started off cleaning houses, then went on to become a typist at the Town Hall in Bromley, ending up as a legal secretary for a local firm of solicitors.

Women of her generation and the generations before her had to fight for everything, to have any voice at all. Life was a struggle. Period.

My life? Well it couldn't be more different. When I was at school however, I remember the careers talks we had – Secretary, Nurse or Teacher. University? Why would you want to do that? Surely you're just finding something to do until you get married and have children?

I didn't realise it then but I was a bit of a maverick. Back in 1977 entrepreneurs didn't really exist in my mindset or vocabulary, and certainly becoming one wasn't on the agenda of the careers talks at an all-girls Grammar School! I always wanted to do the opposite of what people expected of me. Yes I did leave school (on a Friday) to immediately start working as a Secretary in London (the following Monday), but I always managed to find myself doing all sorts of other things apart from what I was paid to do in whatever job I had. I was never backward in coming forward to make my presence felt and volunteered for all sorts of things. If what I wanted to do didn't exist, I invented a reason why it was imperative and talked them into letting me do it.

Eventually twelve years later, at the age of twenty nine, I became self-employed. I went to a conference in London where five women who had started their own businesses were speaking. The final woman to bound onto the stage had started her own style and image company. 'That's it,' I thought, 'that's what I want to do.'

So I went to see her and decided to train. By the end of my training I felt as though I could conquer the world. She made me believe in myself in a way no-one had ever done and I knew then that I wanted other women to feel the way I did, and I would do everything I could to ensure that happened.

I was asked recently what had motivated me to train to be a Style Consultant. My answer was immediate.

As a teenager I had been very overweight – I used my weight as a way to hide from the world and everything that was going on around me, but as a result I was bullied a lot, not particularly at school, but very much so out of school. If I ever went out with my school friends, any boys we were with used to taunt me and then ignore me. I was never validated as a female by my father, so didn't really have much self-esteem in my adolescent years. I therefore saw style consultancy as a way to instil the belief in ALL women that they are beautiful, gorgeous, sexy and fabulous – whatever their age, dress size, budget or lifestyle. I was determined, as I still am, that NO woman will ever doubt her own magnificence for a second, I never want any woman to go through the torment of my experience from my teenage years through to my late twenties.

My teenage years were challenging. My father didn't really want to see me, he had remarried and was fully involved in his new relationship. My step-mother wasn't particularly keen on having a step-daughter, and made that obvious! I went through my teenage years believing I was never pretty, clever or slim enough to be loved. As a result I become more overweight – in an attempt to become invisible, I then became anorexic and started to self-harm. Any boy who did show an interest in me I went along with, because I felt 'grateful' for the attention, believing I wasn't worthy of male interest. The result was that in my early twenties I married a man a lot older than me who was a controlling bully, a passive aggressive and reinforced all the negative beliefs I held about myself. Luckily I still had sufficient belief, however small and however deeply buried, that after three and a half years I realised I deserved better and left. With nothing. Just my clothes and whatever of my self-esteem I had remaining.

I got involved with another man very quickly, before I had spent any time healing myself, and within a year I had left London and moved to Southampton. We married. I had married another version of my first husband and my father. It took me to the age of thirty one to recognise this and, once again, I left with nothing.

I ran a business with my husband so in twenty four hours lost my relationship, a roof over my head and my job. I just about hung onto my mental and physical health but at times that was also hanging in the balance. I eventually moved back to our marital home as he moved back to London, he kept the business and I kept the house, just as the house prices crashed, so I ended up losing my home.

I took a job as a Secretary at Hampshire County Council and continued my style work at weekends. During the week in the evenings I left the office where I worked as a Secretary and went to another office block to clean it. I did whatever it took to pay the bills and reclaim my life.

My boss at the council sent me on a women's self-development programme and at the end they asked me if I would like to train to be a trainer. So I then trained. I left Southampton in 1995 and moved back to Kent, started work in the City and told my employers I ran self development programmes for women, would they be interested? They were. So I spent the next five years doing that, with women flying in from all over Eastern Europe to attend the programmes. I also tackled the issue of gender diversity within the bank and headed up a task force to do something about the inequality. In 1999 I left the bank and started working for a not-for-profit organisation where I account managed forty organisations from the private, public and education sectors and supported them with gender diversity issues. I continued to run my style business for private clients at the weekends and ran lunchtime and evening courses on style and personal branding for other City employees during the week.

During my five years as an Account Manager I had the privilege to work with some amazing women across all sectors. All strong, independent, feisty, smart, funny, but very few of them where they should have been within that organisation. When it came down to it, they held themselves back, worried they would be seen as 'too pushy' 'aggressive' or 'ball breakers'. The ones that did push themselves forward, on the whole rejected a lot of their femininity, as they saw that was the only way to succeed, in the process annoying men and alienating women. Something had to change.

In 2004 I went back to being full-time self-employed running my own training company to tackle the issue of women's lack of self -belief and confidence. I also trained to be an Executive Coach as many clients had asked to work with me one-to-one.

What has made me sad over the years is the division that appears to be getting wider by the year between career women and the organisations that employ them. Employment law has changed, women have considerably more rights now than my mother's generation, but women are still 'fighting'. Or believing they need to. Organisations are constantly portrayed as the 'bad guys', not doing enough, being 'beaten up' by external opinion, taken to court for doing the wrong thing. In truth, the majority of organisations I've worked with want to do the right thing, but they are always presented with the problem and no-one has presented them with the solution.

Yes, organisations have a duty to the women they employ. But you know what? Women have a duty too – to themselves and their employers, whether the employer is a company, or yourself if you run your own business. Women have a duty to be accountable and responsible for their own development, their own confidence and self -belief and their own attitude to life and themselves.

The way forward is NOT in blame – we've had enough of the blame culture to last a lifetime. Collaboration is now the way forward with everyone working together to create a better future. As women we are naturally brilliant at collaboration, we are the best at nurturing, pouring oil on troubled water and looking after others.

It was at the age of thirty one, at the breakdown of my second marriage, that I then started my journey of self-discovery, taking control and ownership and healing. It took me another four years to confront my father, but when I did, he responded positively (after sulking for three months and not talking to me) and we started to build a good, solid relationship.

What I recognised was that to blame, myself or anyone else, was a waste of time and energy. Both my parents did the best job they could with the skill set they had at the time. My dad wasn't perfect, far from it, but his behaviour was a direct result of the upbringing he had had. It wasn't his fault. I could stay in 'blame and anger' but the only person suffering was me.

I noticed my life changed once I stopped blaming my dad for stuff. Our fathers represent our first relationship with the opposite sex, and can mould all future relationships, whether these are personal or professional. When I took control of my inner emotions and related to him from my powerful, assertive and feminine inner core, our relationship was totally transformed and we were the best of friends until his death in 2010. It was easy to go through many years passing the buck and not taking responsibility for 'me'. When I managed to stand firm and get over myself, the path was clear for authenticity in every area of my life.

Trust me, if I can do it, so can you. There aren't many life experiences I haven't had:

A troubled upbringing
Struggling with my weight
Overcoming anorexia
Divorce
Death
Financial struggle (just avoiding bankruptcy)
Losing my home (quite a few times as a child and three times as an adult)
Bullying
Growing up with a lack of self-belief and low self-esteem
Dysfunctional relationships with the opposite sex

I've overcome them all, each time stronger and more resilient and without losing 'me'. In fact, each time 'me' has become more strongly embedded and my essence has flourished. I am proud of who I am today, I look in the mirror every morning and like the person looking back at me – she's a good woman!

Let's start to honour and celebrate YOU. You're also a good woman, someone to be proud of and someone to respect and admire. Onto Chapter Two then – your turn.

Part Two
Who Are You
On The Outside?

Chapter Two
Your Personal Brand

'Don't compromise yourself. You are all you've got.'
Janis Joplin

Be authentic.

Let's start by looking at the essence of who you are, how much power you have in being authentic with your femininity, because:

There will always be more power in being a woman than there will ever be in trying to behave like a man.

As I mentioned in the previous chapter, the need to fight to the same degree as our female ancestors is no longer appropriate. Being truly authentic as women, and making the most of the amazing qualities we possess in bucket-loads will take us far further, with considerably more ease, than trying to emulate the testosterone aggressiveness of men. Which isn't to say that they are wrong, they're not, men are simply being who they are, and we need to be who we are.

What I want you to do is fully embrace your wonderful femininity, step into your full female power and truly own your space and place in the world, stand tall and be proud, REALLY PROUD. Women are just the most incredible human beings, our compassion, negotiation skills, communication prowess, nurturing ability, empowering leadership and management style and all-round fabulousness makes us hard to beat in the working arena and all women need to start believing in themselves and their innate abilities with every fibre of their bodies.

WHEN THE GOING GETS TOUGH, IT'S THE
WOMEN WHO GET GOING!

Let's face it, we don't expect men to behave like women do we? And men don't expect us to behave like them. We're different for a reason. Diversity of style and personality will always make a team, department, company, family-unit stronger, not weaker. The way for us to succeed is *not* to try and be equal – the real meaning of that would make us just like the men. We are not. We're not better than men, men are not better than us, we are simply different. And the moment we accept that and embrace the skills, personalities and amazingness that we were born with, the easier life will become.

My grandmother was a wonderful example of strength and femininity. She brought up four girls (my mum and her three sisters) on her own in the 1930s, very unusual in those days. She was a concert pianist and played at The Wigmore Halls, stood as a Liberal Councillor for Bromley, Kent and was a Homeopath and refused to have her girls vaccinated – quite something for those times. She died when I was two, so sadly I never got to know her well, something I have always regretted, I have had to make do with the stories my mum told me about her. She was always soft, feminine, welcoming, empowering and nurturing, yet stood firmly in her strength and power, wouldn't be swayed from her values and had a clear focus about what she stood for and what she wouldn't tolerate.

Who are you?

What would you like to project about yourself to the outside world? How do you want people to see you? *Who are you?*

If I were to ask your colleagues/friends/family about you, what would they say?

....

....

....

What are the three most important things about you that you would like people to understand about your personal brand – what you stand for in the world?

1..

2..

3..

How effectively do you think you currently convey these to everyone with your behaviour and visual impact?

Score yourself 1 – 10, with 1 being badly and 10 being perfect

Is there room for improvement? If so, what do you need to do to improve the number?

....

....

....

....

....

....

....

Who do you admire?

For me, my ancestors have really inspired me, my grandmother I've already talked about. My great grandmother, quite a few times back – the 1700s to be precise – was the first great woman in my line of amazing great women. She was a heroine of the Jacobite Rising in 1745. At the tender age of twenty, and as wife to the Chief of Mackintosh, who remained in England, Anne took up the cause of Bonnie Prince Charlie and inspected the clan regiment before it left for Stirling, selecting MacGillvray of Dunmaglas as Colonel. The Jacobite force moved back to the north and the prince arrived at Moy, the seat of the Mackintosh clan, on 16 February 1746 where he was received by Anne, the Lady Mackintosh. A real Boudicca.

Coming to the present day, there are many women who inspire me, both in my personal life and in the media. I have an incredible friend, Rosie, who was seventy in 2011 and continues to re-invent herself, she has run her own massage school, is a Hypnotherapist, trained to be a Voice-over Artist, has done modelling (last year!) and grows her own vegetables on her allotment. I just hope I have her energy and verve for life at seventy. She is a truly amazing and in-spirational woman.

I have always admired Oprah Winfrey, a real example of female leadership at its absolute best. She is one of the richest and most respected women in North America, and possibly globally, she is known for her nurturing and embracing style with all her employees, whilst remaining true to her message and who she is in her profes-sional life. She has never been shy in sharing her life challenges with us all, expressing her humility and approachability.

Karren Brady is another one. Talk about being a female leader in a male environment. You don't get much more testosterone-fuelled than the football pitch. Yet she has retained her beautiful femininity, is strong in her power, and is one seriously sexy mamma! She also complements wonderfully the male energy of Alan Sugar and Nick on *The Apprentice*. I love her. Just the most perfect example and role model. She writes a wonderful article every month for a women's magazine which I read regularly, her down-to-earth attitude and lovely sense of humour radiate out with every word.

Who inspires/has inspired you along the way. What is it about them that inspires you? How do they act, speak, look, 'be'?

....

....

....

....

How do you manage your image?

What am I talking about here? Just the way you dress? Not entirely, although that does play a large part. Your image, or personal brand, encompasses everything about how you relate to the world and everyone in it. It's your body language, voice – tone, pitch, volume (more about that in Chapter Ten), your dress, your behaviour-style and communication skills, in essence, our non-verbal communication.

In 1964 Professor Albert Mehrabian conducted research on how people receive messages. A summary of his findings are that the words we actually say represent about seven per cent of the message we give, with the remaining ninety three per cent dependant upon our tone of voice and facial expression. The words that we use are, of course, vitally important, but it's how they are communicated that carries more power and influence. This is why text messages and emails are potentially so dangerous – we are only communicating seven per-cent of our message effectively, so the text/email is received completely dependant on the state of mind of the person reading it, not the state of mind of the person who sent it.

This creates room for potential conflict and misunderstanding, which has, and will, continue to happen. Be very careful how you phrase your text and email messages, they may come back and bite you on the bum!

I'd like you to visualise the highest and best version of YOU.

• What do you look like?
• How are you dressed?
• How are you communicating to people?
• How are you being received?
• What are your relationships like – personal and business?

Capture your thoughts and visions here.

....

....

....

....

....

....

Are you creating your own obstacles?

Really think – are you putting up any barriers to achieving a personal brand that reflects all your skills, talents and values to the world? If you are, what do you need to do to rectify the situation – is it something tangible (buying a new wardrobe for example), something internal (giving yourself a kick up the backside and stopping the negative self-talk), something constructive (looking at your behaviour-style and learning a new way of 'being').

What do you need to create?
Is it time/money/belief?
And what's in it for you?
What is your reward?

Whatever it is, capture it here. I need to ...

....

....

....

....

....

By when?

....

OK, so now you've started to have a look 'inside' and have begun to ignite those deeply embedded unconscious thoughts and bring them to the forefront of your mind, in the next chapter I'm going to talk you through how you can explore some practical steps to manifest your beauty and start to shine in the world.

Chapter Three
Your Personal Style

'A bird doesn't sing because it has an answer, it sings because it has a song.'
Maya Angelou

This chapter is about how I work one-to-one with women to help them create their visual personal brand, the nuts-and-bolts of the style work I do. It's about how to communicate your uniqueness and beauty with your clothes and personal style.

Colour

I always start off with colour when I work with a client, it's the obvious and logical first step in establishing your personal style. Some style consultants will work with tonal words – cool, warm, bright, muted, and some work with seasons – spring, summer, autumn, winter. Both are fine and both mean the same things. I happen to work with the seasons as I find this is better for my clients, it's much easier to visualise a copper-leaf autumn in your mind's eye than the words 'warm, deep and muted'. And I would much rather tell my client she's a fabulous jewelled winter than tell her she's cold and sharp!

But first things first, the history of colour and how the Colour Wheel came into being. It's always good to know the 'science' behind the system, it really helps clients to understand what I'm doing, the process I go through and why, and for them to see how it's working on them and why they are seeing what they are seeing.

Going right back to the beginning of time, the word 'colour' did not exist in language, but the colours recreated by people living then were: red, blue, green and yellow. These represented what they saw around them – red was fire, blue was the sky, green was grass, trees and plants, and yellow was the sun. The names of these colours, however did not exist.

Moving forward to 1930s the Colour Wheel that is used by Style Consultants today was introduced, although at that time it did not have the application it does today in fashion, it was used solely for architecture and design.

Walter Gropius, the founder of The Bauhaus School of Art and Architecture in Berlin in 1930s discovered that although his students painted the same scene, the scenes often looked different. The sky was blue, the grass was green and the poppies were red, but they were different shades and shapes. As all his students were looking at the same thing when they painted, he wanted to find out why their interpretation differed from person to person.

He commissioned one of his students, Johannes Itten, to do research into colour. This Itten did, and produced a huge tome on the subject. The essence of his research was that he discovered that all colours have a temperature. All colours are made up of the three primary colours of red, yellow and blue. Some shades of colour have a stronger blue pigment and some shades of colour have a stronger yellow pigment. If a shade of colour has a stronger yellow pigment it is 'warm', if a shade of colour has a stronger blue pigment it is 'cool'.

This is the first division of the Colour Wheel – the temperature of a colour. Whilst every colour will fall into one of these categories, so will every person. Everyone's skin is made up of the three primary colours of red, yellow and blue. Some people have a stronger yellow pigment to their skin and some have a stronger blue pigment to their skin. In colour analysis, we say the opposite to what we can see.

For example, if a person has a stronger yellow pigment to their skin, they are termed 'Blue Based'. This means that the blue base of their skin-tone is not visible, but the yellow tone is. If these people wear colours that also have a strong yellow pigment, they are then adding yellow to yellow and exacerbating the yellow on their skin by pushing it out; they end up looking muddy, jaundiced and ill. People with a predominant yellow tone to their skin need to wear shades of colour that have a dominant blue tone to them, hence bringing out the 'blue base' of their skin-tone that cannot be seen and balancing the skin-tone.

If a person has a stronger blue pigment to their skin, they are termed 'Yellow Based'. This means that the yellow base of their skin-tone is not visible, but the blue tone is. If these people wear colours that also have a strong blue pigment, they are adding blue to blue and exacerbating the blue on their skin by pushing it out, they end up looking sharp and cold, with red cheeks, blue lips and circles under their eyes. People with a predominant blue tone to their skin need to wear shades of colour that have a dominant yellow tone to them, hence bringing out the 'yellow base' of their skin tone that cannot be seen and balancing the skin-tone.

The second division of the Colour Wheel was discovered by another Bauhaus student, Kandinski. He discovered that not only does colour have a temperature, it also has a shape.

Some colours are soft, muted and hazy with curved lines and some colours are clear, bright and sharp with straight lines and angles.

Hence we get the four divisions of the Colour Wheel, split into sections and seasons as follows:

Winter   **Cool, clear and bright**

Summer   **Cool, soft and muted**

Autumn   **Warm, soft and muted**

Spring   **Warm, clear and bright**

People with a dominant blue pigment need to warm their skin up, so they are likely to be Autumn or Spring. People with a dominant yellow pigment need to cool their skin down, so they are likely to be Winter or Summer.

What is really crucial to point out here is that everyone can wear every colour. It's the shade of colour that's important. There are roughly nine million shades of colour out there, we all have about a quarter of those that we can wear successfully, so there should always be something in the shops to suit you whatever time of year you go shopping!

Everyone can wear blue, red, pink, green, yellow etc. It is about identifying the temperature and shape of these colours to perfectly complement your skin-tone, hair and eyes. This is the true heart of colour analysis.

Face, personality and colour

We are all individuals and operate uniquely in the world, however there are certain similarities that we may share with others. An example of these similarities can be our facial appearances and how that links to our potential range of colours.

The four facial appearances are:

Yang   Strength – lots of contrast, strong features, straight/angled jaw line, more olive skin-tones

Yin   Softness – paler skin, smaller features, delicate colouring, soft outline to the face

Gamine   Naughty – cheeky, mischievous look, sparkly eyes, big smile

Natural   Outdoorsy – sporty, tomboy

This is not cast in stone, but generally the following will be likely:

Winters have predominantly **Yang** facial features

Summers have predominantly **Yin** facial features

Springs have predominantly **Gamine** facial features

Autumns have predominantly **Natural** facial features

Over 2,400 years ago the Greek philosopher Hippocrates studied human behaviours and produced a theory that characterised people as being one of four temperaments, these are:

Phlegmatic   **Slow-moving**

Melancholic   **A worrier**

Sanguine   **Animated**

Choleric   **Assertive**

Bringing this up-to-date, the four colour seasons fit into this theory.

Summers tend to be Phlegmatic in temperament

Winters tend to be Melancholic in temperament

Springs tend to be Sanguine in temperament

Autumns tend to be Choleric in temperament

Summers

Summers tend to be more reserved than other people, but they really love people. They love to know what's going on and can be quite 'fact' driven. They have a tendency to be hard on themselves. Summers can struggle with change slightly more than other people. If a Summer disagrees with you or doesn't want to do something, they will always be charming about it, they don't like conflict and will try to avoid it if they can. They may need convincing about a new idea or concept, but once you've got them onboard they are likely to be your strongest supporter.

As Summers love people, they are very good at getting involved with group activities and make very good team-players. Even though they may not actively promote themselves into leadership roles, if they find themselves in that position they do it brilliantly as they possess great ability in their communication style and they have a strong ability to remain calm under pressure.

A Summer is likely to process their thoughts before speaking and when they do speak it is usually with a soft voice, their overall character and persona is gentle, which naturally acts as a magnet for others. They are very understanding which results in people feeling secure to confide in them and tell them things they wouldn't tell other people.

Summers are more likely to observe within group situations and be quieter than others, they have excellent listening skills.

Some of their characteristics:

Speak quietly

Listen intensely

Appreciative of clear facts and written information

If they disagree with you they will be polite and charming

Slower than others to embrace change and new ideas

If they are feeling comfortable they will ask questions, if they're not they will shut down

Winters

Winter people are very good at motivating themselves and can always be depended on. They have a very self-assured presence, they are born leaders and will not shy away from assuming positions of authority. They have the ability to look at the bigger picture and can delegate very well. They can be quite single-minded and tunnel-visioned – once they set their sights on something, very little will distract them.

They can be quite dramatic with their personality and make wonderful actors and are brilliant in law – particularly as barristers as this gives them the opportunity to 'perform' under pressure, however they can take themselves very seriously and may not always be as 'in control' or as comfortable as they appear to everyone else.

Winters may have a tendency to over-think things rather than going with the flow, which can result in being sensitive to the opinion of others. Their inner-talk (what they say when they talk to themselves) is likely to be more constant and louder than anyone else's, which may mean they appear slightly distant to the people who are looking at them, they have a habit of frowning when they are thinking.

Some of their characteristics:

Love clear direction

Usually prefer to complete one task before starting another

Are likely to be perfectionists

May not believe in themselves as much as they should

Like reassurance from others

Springs

Spring people are bubbly, exuberant, lovers of life and always see the glass as half full. They tend to laugh a lot and have no problem being the centre of attention. Their face will light up when they're happy, they are great fun to be around – a bit like very bouncy two-year-olds! As leaders they are brilliant at motivating people with their energy and enthusiasm and their optimism is inspiring. They are very positive people who are very good at trouble-shooting and finding possibilities in situations where others struggle, however they may not be the tidiest people in the world and will need someone who can keep them focussed and on track.

Springs are very charming, make great networkers because of their love of life and enjoyment in being around many people, they also have a wonderful ability to make small-talk on any subject at the drop of a hat. Sometimes, though, they may open their mouth before they engage their brain! This makes them at times unpredictable and their sense of humour may not be to everyone's taste.

Springs are very practical and prefer to 'get on with it' rather than discuss the ins-and-outs of a situation, they have energy levels that are in excess of most human beings and quite often will have their intelligence hugely underestimated by others.

They will take risks others would not and love the excitement of the next big thing, but they may forget to think things through and plan ahead appropriately. Their ability to take risks makes for a strong leadership style, but they would be advised to have a strong team underneath them who are able to keep them on track and help them to be finishers.

Some of their characteristics:

They get very excited about life

Talk a lot

They forgive mistakes more readily than others

Are very adaptable and flexible to change

May leap from one idea to the next and need help making decisions

Autumns

If you are looking for the strong goal-setters of this world, look no further, Autumns are your women! They are motivated, very intense, incredibly strong-willed and can be extremely direct in the way they communicate.

Because of their organisational ability, their independence and self-discipline, they make excellent leaders, exceptional businesswomen and entrepreneurs. However, their natural dominance in groups may mean they overpower discussions and overwhelm more sensitive people in their presence. Autumns are quick to correct anyone who may not come up to their standard of performance, their high integrity and desire for the best are excellent leadership qualities, but at times may need to be 'softened' to allow others to make mistakes. They can be very quick-tempered and may need to acquire people-skills if they are in positions of management or leadership.

They have the ability to organise any project and will have completed the task while others are still debating the best way to tackle it. They are headstrong, but once you have them onboard they will promote a cause or project with total dedication, focus and energy.

Autumns generally make decisions very quickly and will not suffer fools gladly, they get irritated by procrastination, they can easily become workaholics, as work is exhilarating for them and can provide an outlet for their energy and drive. They need support to relax and take life less seriously.

They are very loyal friends and supporters, Autumns are the true Amazonians of the world, they will fight your corner to the end and woe betide anyone who gets in their way.

Some of their characteristics:

Very self-assured

Dislikes rambling – always get to the point with Autumns

Understand concepts well and will ask pertinent questions

Usually act on advice immediately

Love quick results, not very good at waiting, patience is definitely NOT one of their virtues

What are your personal colours?

Short Test

1. Face the palm of your hand up, and look at your forearm in natural light. Does your skin have a pink or yellow undertone, and mark the answer below.

A) Pink undertone ☐ **B)** Yellow undertone ☐

2. Test with the colour of metal. Use gold and silver, either pieces of fabric if you have some or pieces of gold and silver jewellery. Separately hold up each to your face - which colour brings a healthier glow to the skin?

A) Gold ☐   **B)** Silver ☐

3. Do you tan easily?

A) No ☐   **B)** Yes ☐

4. Which lipstick are you more likely to buy?

A) An orangey red or brown shade   ☐

B) A rosy red or pink shade   ☐

5. Which colours do you prefer?

A) Terracotta, Moss Green. Saffron Yellow, Bronze,
   Turquoise Blue ☐

B) Rose Pink, Emerald Green, Acid Yellow, Grey,
   Cornflower Blue ☐

If you answers three or more questions with 'A', your skin-tone is most likely cool. If three or more of your answers were 'B', your skin-tone is most likely warm.

This is just a quick exercise though, and it is very difficult to self-analyse as it is almost impossible to be objective with ourselves. You will probably know what season you are, definitely if you've had a consultation and have your Colour Fan already, most people will surround everything they look at in their seasonal colours – they buy their friends/partner/children presents and clothes in those colours, they may well decorate their home in those colours and even buy their loo roll in those colours! What most people don't do, however, is put the colours on themselves. Every photograph of me as child you see me dressed in wonderful summer colours of rose pink, lavender, cornflower blue and primrose yellow – my mum was a Summer and she dressed me in all her colours. She got it half right – muted, but I need warm-muted colours (Autumn) not cool-muted colours (Summer).

I would strongly recommend that if you haven't had your colours done that you find a style consultant you feel comfortable with, can trust and are attracted to and go through the process. A full consultation will take anything from an hour to an hour-and-a-half and should include your make-up colours as well as your clothes. You will also be given your Colour Fan. I always personalise a client's Colour Fan and show her exactly how to interpret her range of colours and how to pull together the selection for business, casual and evening. Make sure you get the full service and information, just knowing what season you are isn't enough.

The psychology of colour

Different colours have long symbolised different objects or emotions. At the same time, studies have shown that colours have different psychological effects on people. You may wish to wear a certain colour or colour combination in order to create the desired impact.

Red

Symbolises fire and blood, and stands for excitement and physical strength. It has a great deal of energy and intensity, and can also create a very romantic, passionate or dramatic mood. Whilst seen as the colour of energy it can also be seen as a colour of aggression so should be worn with care in the business world. Be aware of the impact you will have wearing red and decide if it's appropriate to the situation. It represents the Base Chakra – foundation, grounding, energy. If you want the power that red will give you without it being visible to others – wear it as underwear!

Pink and Peach

These are delicate, feminine, compassionate and calming, and they project less energy than red.

Orange

Orange stands for fire and sunlight. Orange is like red, but toned down in intensity. It can reflect friendliness and liveliness. It represents the Sacral Chakra – joy and fun.

Yellow

This is the colour representing sunshine. It indicates radiance, warmth and receptivity and brings out an approachable and cheerful look. It represents the Solar Plexus Chakra – deep emotions and feelings.

Green

This colour induces a feeling of stability, balance, naturalness and tranquility. When used near the face, green can also create tension and drama. It represents the Heart Chakra – relationships and love.

Blue

This colour represents the sky and water. The light blues are calming, while the dark blues such as navy, give off a feeling of power and authority. It represents the Throat Chakra – communication, so a great colour to wear if you need to deliver a presentation.

Purple

This stands for the mystical, sensitivity, uniqueness, and artistry. It represents the highest authority colour because in the past it was the most expensive colour to reproduce, therefore unless you were of a certain financial standing within society, you couldn't afford to have purple clothes. This is still with us today, the high echelons of royalty, the law and the church all use deep purple. It represents the Third Eye Chakra – inner-seeing and knowledge.

Brown

This is associated with the ground, dirt and earth, and it creates a strong feeling of comfort, sincerity and casualness.

Black

This stands for the night, power, mystery and dignity. Because of its versatility, it has been one of the most well-worn fashion colours.

Grey

This is a neutral that is not based on any hue. It is a mixture of black and white. It indicates peace, calmness, reliability and conservatism. Dark grey signifies power and authority.

White

This is symbolic of light. It stands for purity, cleanliness, innocence and goodness. It represents the Crown Chakra – spirituality.

Using this in the real world

So why is all this important in your life? Let's face it, you've got this far wearing a black suit, white shirt, black court shoes and minimal make-up, who needs to introduce rose pink and burnt orange into their wardrobes for heavens sake! What's that phrase – if it ain't broke, don't fix it?

Fair point.

But this book is about you being your true authentic self, not a manual in how to look like everyone else. Why be part of the crowd when you could stand out and be even more amazing? And, not to put too fine a point on it black, and white, may not suit you. Plus black and white is what the men do, do you *really* want to be like them, or would you prefer to have your own unique power and visual impact?

Do you live in a city or large town far away from nature? Do you ever long for green fields, the sea, a wood? Cities can be the most wonderful, vibrant, energetic places, which is why we are drawn to them to work, they give us an injection of energy and life and get the adrenaline going. But after a while that environment can also become stressful. The reason is very little in a city is in harmony as far as colour is concerned, the contrasting bright lights all fighting for supremacy, the jagged buildings thrusting manfully into the sky proving they are the strongest, the proudest. Eventually that starts to drain us of our energy and it becomes a struggle to survive and to have a voice when you're surrounded by such noise. Noise doesn't have to be what we hear, noise can also be what we see, it gets in the way of our inner calm and balance.

Our eyes and brain are always seeking harmony and calm, this is why we often long for nature. To walk among trees, flowers, meadows, see the sea etc. Nature is where we can rest our circuits, regain our balance, recharge our batteries and prepare ourselves for the time ahead.

Nature is perfect. I'd like you to imagine in your mind's eye two flowers – a daffodil and a rose (it doesn't matter what colour the rose is). Once you have the image of these flowers in your mind, I'd like you to imagine the flower of the daffodil with the stem and leaves of the rose, and the flower of the rose with the stem and leaves of the daffodil. Does it work? No, it doesn't, it 'feels' wrong even though you can't physically see them. As soon as you visualise the flowers in the right place, harmony is restored and you relax.

Well, guess what? You are part of nature, and you are perfect! Fabulous. The problem is, most people will work against their own perfection. I could take any child up to the age of about six or seven and leave them in a clothes shop. They would very quickly pick out the colours of clothes that are right for them. We are all born with this inner knowing, but of course children don't buy their own clothes, they have them chosen for them, and by the time that child is old enough to buy for themselves, so many other messages have been absorbed that the inner knowing they were born with has long gone.

You were that child, you were born knowing how perfect you are, but over the years other people have taken you off track, and now there is so much choice out there it can be totally overwhelming. So many messages from so many places, for instance our parents, friends, the media, 'celebrities' etc.

But think about how restful and calming it is to look at and be in nature. Think about how potentially stressful it is to be surrounded by visual chaos. Which visual image would you like to project to the world? Part of being authentic is in ensuring you present the real 'you'. The 'you' that is in harmony with yourself. By default that makes you easier to look at, therefore more approachable, a better communicator and you draw people towards you like a magnet rather than run the risk of pushing them away. A good leader has natural charisma, they are the people others want to follow, to be like, they inspire greatness in everyone else.

What are you currently? A leader or a follower?

If you are authentic it allows others to be themselves, to be true to who they are, people relax around you, perform better, are more loyal and less stressed. And all this by getting the right colours – who would have thought!

Knowing the range of colours to suit your particular skin-tone is fabulous, but that's only half the story. It really helps if you also know what shapes your clothes need to be to best reflect your body and inner personality. Only then can you truly present yourself with total authenticity and really glow. So in the next chapter, I'll talk you through Style and Clothing Personalities.

Chapter Four
Your Inner Personality

'The future belongs to those who believe in the beauty of their dreams.'
Eleanor Roosevelt

Establishing your place on the Colour Wheel is fantastic, but that's only half the story. It's really important that to be truly authentic with your visual image, that you honour your body too.

Honour my WHAT? Are you kidding? Have I told you you're perfect? I think so, but I'll say it again anyway:

YOU'RE PERFECT!

To discover your true, unique style it's vital that you honour both your outer body and your inner personality. Not to do so would mean you only dress the 'shell' of who you are − the outside. That simply won't do. It's crucial that you celebrate the *whole* of you, the very essence of you as well as dressing that gorgeous shape and wonderful body.

Did you know that every woman on the planet is beautiful? I know. What I see on a regular basis, however, are beautiful women 'pretending' to be plain. Women seem to have a self destruct button that they press the moment I tell them how fabulous they are, they come up with all sorts of excuses as to why they couldn't possibly agree with me:

I'm too old
I'm too young
I'm too fat
I'm too thin
I'm too short
I'm too tall
I can't afford it

It's too scary

What would other people think?

I haven't got time

So, when I work with clients on their style we look at all aspects of who they are, their lifestyle, the appropriate visual image for every aspect of their lives, what they want to project to the world. Part of that process is discovering your Clothing Personality, taking into account both your outer shape and inner personality. Let me explain the different personalities and give you examples, you may well recognise yourself and quite possibly other people too.

There are six main categories, which can all be mixed and matched. Sometimes a person is just one personality, which means they are the same inside as they are outside, rare but it does happen. More often people are a combination of two. Here they are.

Dramatic

Queen of the Night, Wicked Queen, Witches, Ice Queens, Wicked Stepmothers, Spiders, Serpents and Warriors

Dramatics have very angular bodies and faces and are often taller than average. They are hard to ignore, they can be publicity seekers and attention getters. They can impose their will, be controlling, formidable, unapproachable and tend to take over in situations. In social and business life they are the risk takers. They appear to take up space whenever they enter a room. Dramatic women will rarely be described as pretty, rather they are 'stunning' and 'striking'. Their personal space will likely be twice everyone else's, they keep people at arms length.

But my goodness, they get things done! They are in truth very feeling people, but because of their natural reserve, you really have to get to know a Dramatic well before they have built up sufficient trust in you to show their vulnerability.

Think Meryl Streep in *The Devil Wears Prada* and Cruella de Ville in *101 Dalmatians*.

Classic

Regal, Stately, Head Girl, Prefect, Head Teacher, In Charge, Very Responsible, Looks Expensive

Classics tend to have straight bodies, but with far less angles than a Dramatic. Everything about a Classic is even, evenly spaced bodies, symmetrical faces. They have a natural authority and easily take charge of situations. They engender trust in others very quickly. They tend to live by the rules, their body-language is very composed and calm, they really don't like clutter, preferring order and neatness in every area of their lives.

Like Dramatics, they can sometimes be difficult to get close to, not being naturally at ease with small talk and what they deem to be insignificant conversation. Classic women are naturally elegant and move with grace.

Think the late Grace Kelly.

Natural

Adventurers, Entrepreneurial Pirates, Gypsies, Cowgirls, Tomboys

Naturals have easy movement to their bodies, they need clothes that have fluidity, they can't take structure and severe tailoring. Their bodies are generally soft straight and they look best in layers and material that has drape and flow. Naturals are not great at tidiness. In fact they really don't see clutter at all. Not the best partners for a Classic. They operate to their optimum in environments where they can take risks, push the boundaries, try out new ideas, experiment and definitely be different from the crowd, they create the vision, others follow. Generally very charismatic people.

Think the late Anita Roddick.

Gamine

Boyish, Cheeky, Pixie, Elfin-like, Quick and Nippy Movement, Naughty and Very Perky!

Gamine women tend to have straight and sometimes sharp straight bodies, but are much smaller than the previous three personalities. They tend to be shorter with a smaller bone structure. Quite boyish in their shape. Again will push the boundaries and definitely do things 'their way'. Generally they hate following the crowd and celebrate their individuality. They are like little terriers, they rarely let something go until they get it to work, they are very demanding on themselves and therefore can be quite challenging to work for. On the opposite, they can be the life and soul of a party and great fun to be around. They appreciate structure, order and neatness.

Think Coco Chanel.

Ingénue

Forever Young, Youthful, Pretty, Delicate, Precise

This is quite possibly the strongest of the clothing personalities. Most ingénue women have a core of steel running through them. But because on the outside they look very fragile, men automatically want to wrap them in cotton wool and protect them. These are women who seriously do not need to be protected and, as a result, most ingénue women will deny their innate femininity. They may view it as a weakness, not a strength, where, in fact, it is their greatest asset. They prefer structure to their clothes, similar to the Gamine, they are usually shorter and smaller in bone structure than the average woman. If they honour their ingénue they are one of the most devastatingly powerful women around.

Think Goldie Hawn (who does honour her ingénue and does it brilliantly).

Romantic

Sexy, Curvy, Voluptuous, Tactile, Luscious, Hour-glass, Bedroom-eyes!

Romantic women have curvy bodies, usually a larger bust, smaller waist and bigger hips, the true hour-glass figures. Their personal space is usually half everyone else's, they can be your best friend within minutes and will likely have told you their life story. They touch people a lot while they are talking and love very tactile material. They are great 'people' people, very focussed on making others feel good about themselves, very generous with their time and attention. They need clothes that hug their bodies, nothing too rigid in structure.

Think Marilyn Monroe.

Once you have identified where you are on the above scale (remembering most people are a combination of two) it makes life a lot easier. Both in terms of finding the right styles to flatter you and show you off to your best advantage, as well as the right accessories. It also allows you to relax knowing that you are being the best you can be, it stops you comparing yourself with other women, wishing you were more this or more that, accepting that who you are is absolutely stunning.

I happen to be a Natural Romantic, curvy, very busty, will never ever be a size 0. Whilst I admire from afar the wonderful Chanel Suit, I know that it would make me look like a sack of potatoes. So why go there? But the woman who does look wonderful in the Chanel Suit would look ridiculous in the clothes that make me look gorgeous. This is not about trying to be like someone else, it's about honouring and celebrating YOU.

As with colour, it is very difficult to analyse yourself, but you probably started to recognise yourself in some of the descriptions above.

Again, I would strongly recommend that if you haven't had a session with a Style Consultant that you do so, it is invaluable and a real investment in you and your future.

Your personal image audit

All the information above is not, you'll be relieved to hear, just my opinion. It is all based on history and is very firmly embedded in our subconscious, so deeply that most people are completely unaware that they are being impacted by this information on a daily basis.

What is the first thing you notice about people when you walk into a room of strangers, go to the theatre, cinema etc? Actually, you may be surprised to know that the very first thing we clock is gender – where are the men and where are the women. Once that bit's ticked, we then start to notice the details. This is when it becomes really alive. We probably don't know anything about these people in front of us, but we will all make snap decisions about them there and then. All our decisions will be based on our subconscious making up its mind and sending the message through to our conscious minds – shall we talk to that person or ignore them? Are they trustworthy or do they look a bit 'dodgy'? Do they look friendly or frankly rather intimidating? As we know nothing about these people all these decisions are based on what we see, we have absolutely nothing else to go on, we have no other information at that stage that will help us make up our minds.

Yes, we all know that what's really important is the person inside, who they are, how they operate in the world, their values etc. However when we meet people for the first time (and when they meet us come to that) we have no idea who they are on the inside, and the chances are we may not have time to find out that much about them, all we have to go on to help us make our decisions is what we see when we look at them – what's on the outside – the ninety three per cent of their non-verbal communication.

This goes back to the twelfth century when the Rules of Dress were very strongly in place. If someone broke the Rules of Dress, wore something that was inappropriate to their status in that society, they could be fined a sum of money. This may seem bizarre to us today, but actually on some level this still happens. If we present ourselves in a way that is inappropriate – for the situation, our age, our role, even the weather – we may still get fined, not in terms of money, but perhaps we won't get the job/promotion, we get ostracised at an event (business or social), people ignore us. Have you ever seen that happen to someone? They really got their 'look' wrong, a part of us will want to go and rescue them (a very 'female' reaction) but possibly a bigger part of us will just ignore them because we don't really know what to say or do to make it better, and human beings are hugely judgemental, our love and friendship is very rarely unconditional (unless you're a mother). I know that's a very harsh statement, but it's true. Anyone who says they are not remotely judgemental of anyone else is in denial, it is a natural human reaction.

When was the last time you went to the cinema? What's the usual length of a film nowadays, about two hours? There's usually quite a complex story involved, with many characters, some in the foreground and many in the background, but all relevant to the how the story and film hang together. The people making the film use the power of the Rules of Dress so that the audience watching will make the snap judgements about the characters that they need us to make, in order that we get the plot, understand what's going on and leave the Cinema with the satisfaction of seeing a really good film. All of this information is being absorbed by us on a subconscious level, so never kid yourself that you are immune from judgement by others, none of us are. What you need to do is to ensure, as far as you can, that the judgements from others are positive rather than negative and that you naturally draw people towards you like a magnet rather than repel them.

Many women (particularly in the UK I've noticed) are brought up with the non-permission to look good. One of the internal messages that can be recorded at a very early age and reinforced on a regular basis is that it's 'vain' to spend too much attention on yourself, it's 'silly' and unnecessary, feather-brained, waste of time and money etc. But I would like to challenge that belief and tell you here and now it's nonsense. Please don't believe it any longer if you ever did. Very few things in this life are free, but the way in which we treat other people by our actions is one of them. And part of our actions towards other people is how much time, care and attention we spend on how we put ourselves together visually. It is very rude not to bother, because potentially we are telling everyone who has to look at us for the day that they were not worth the effort.

I'd like to tell you about an experience I had back in 2004. I was working with a large national property company in the UK, working with the Chairman and his Board of Directors (all men by the way). I jointly arranged a day for them to visit two places in London, firstly a school where they could experience the challenges faced by the teachers, and secondly a Mission for the Homeless.

The brief at the Mission was to chat to the people the Mission helped and get to know them and their story. We all went into the dining room and I sat opposite two men. Initially their body language was very closed and passive, looking down, not meeting my eye and no engagement.

Then one of them looked up at me and said, 'You look nice,' in a very accusatory way.
  'Thank you,' I said, 'I was coming to see you.'
  'What do you mean?' he said. To which I replied, 'Any reason why I would take less time with my appearance when I'm coming to see you today, than I did when I was with the Chief Executive yesterday?'
  'So you did that for me?' was his answer.
  'Yes, any reason why I wouldn't bother for you?'
  'No, I suppose not,' came the reply.
  Then his friend looked up and said, 'Pretty isn't she!'
  'Thank you,' I said.

From then on, their whole body-language changed, their shoulders went back, we had eye-contact and they chatted to me for half-an-hour, telling me their story, how they had ended up on the streets, the fact that they had been friends for twenty years on the streets and supported each other. At the end of our time together when we stood up, they both gave me a kiss and said "Thank you". Because what I had said to them by my appearance was that they were worth it, they were worth me getting out of bed in time to do my hair, put on make-up and think about what I was going to wear. Everyone deserves your time and attention, whether that person is on the check-out at your supermarket or your boss. It's polite. Not to do so is impolite. How do you want to be seen and judged by others? As someone who respects other people, no matter who they are, or someone who only thinks of themselves and frankly can't be bothered?

Your visual image is not only telling other people what you think of them, but you are also telling them what you think of yourself.

People will respond to you dependant upon the messages that you give to them about yourself.

• If you don't value yourself – why would anyone else value you?

• If you don't think you're good enough – why would anyone else think you're good enough?

• If you don't think you're worth the time and effort – why would anyone else?

• If you don't believe you can do the job well – why would anyone else trust you?

• If you don't aspire to progress – why would anyone else consider you?

Breaking News :
Women dress their emotions.

Wow! Who would have thought?

Have you ever woken up and had a seriously bad-hair day? And boy, doesn't everyone else know about it. What started off as a bit of a dodgy day quickly descends into total mayhem and chaos, nothing goes your way, everybody is against you, even people you've never met, the train is late because it clearly has a grudge against you and no-one else. Colleagues appear to be particularly difficult and un-cooperative, obviously targeting you to dump all their bad behaviour onto, no-one else is getting that treatment, so it must be you.

Eventually after what seems like an age, you get home, even more grumpy and upset than when you left home in the morning, tired, fed-up, hating yourself and the world, quite possibly having eaten everything that you shouldn't have during the day and hating your-self even more! The diet's been broken, so what's the point? Might as well give up now, after all you knew you'd never stick to it anyway. Obviously you're rubbish, not worthy of the job you have, let alone a more responsible one, quite clearly everyone is better than you, more talented, more confident, more worthy, more popular…

Anything there ringing any bells?

What we give out to the world, we get back. But we probably get it back magnified about ten times. So if you give out negativity about yourself, you'll likely get that mirrored back to you on a much larger scale, thus confirming the negativity you believed about yourself in the first place. A vicious circle and one that really needs to be bro-ken, NOW.

Your visual image will tell the world what you believe about yourself, that you value yourself, you are worthy of attention and respect, you are trustworthy and have confidence in yourself and your abilities. Combined with the remaining part of the ninety three per cent of communication, and what you project is someone who other people need to take notice of, for all the right reasons.

You become a magnet
You become someone other people aspire to be like
You ooze charisma and confidence
You inspire others by your very presence

YOU BECOME A LEADER

I mean a leader of the right way to 'be', a leader of values, courtesy, respect, a beacon for others to follow.

Do you wear a uniform to work? If you've just answered 'no' to that question, I'd like to disagree.

The assumption is that the only uniforms are the recognisable dress of the Armed Forces, the Emergency Services etc. They are not. Uniforms are there to indicate to other people how they are meant to respond to you. The very clear uniforms of the Armed Forces or Emergency Services (particularly uniformed police) do the job excellently. It is, in fact, the uniform that is being saluted, not the person. It is the uniform that indicates to everyone else how they are meant to respond.

Everything you put on is part of your 'uniform'. When you get dressed in the morning, the uniform you wear is how you tell everyone who sees you that day how they are meant to respond to you, how much respect they should show you, should you be saluted or ignored?

When you get up tomorrow morning, and you're out of the shower and standing in front of your wardrobe with nothing on, imagine your body is a blank sheet of paper. Every item of clothing you put on represents a word. When you've finished getting dressed, you've written a sentence. Take a look in the mirror, what sentence have you written about yourself? Is it what you want everyone else to read? Because the moment you step outside your front door, they will read it. Does it make sense? Are all the items you're wearing saying the same thing, or are there any mixed messages that will confuse people? (Shoes that say I'd rather be at the beach, a suit that says I'm the boss and earrings that say I'm going clubbing the moment I leave the office.) If there's any confusion with your sentence and your message, people will waste time trying to figure out who you are, which means they are not listening to what you have to say.

It is very easy to present yourself as a victim or a powerhouse of authority. And however you present yourself is how you will be treated. Which one would you like? To be treated as a victim or a powerhouse of authority?

It really is that simple. We all have choices in life, some of them are major some inconsequential. The choice you make about how you are in the world, what you believe about yourself, how you communicate your values, the respect you show others and yourself and how you intend to be treated, is one of the most important choices of your life.

PLEASE ENSURE YOU MAKE THE RIGHT ONE

Years ago there was a very powerful programme on television. It was about street-crime and mugging. There was one particular young man who had been mugged repeatedly. The producers of the documentary filmed him walking over a bridge in a large city, dressed as he normally was, body-language as it normally was, and asked a group of young offenders who had mugged other people, to watch the film and pick out the person walking in the crowd that they would target to mug. Every one of them picked this young man. When asked why, they said he 'looked like a victim'.

That young man had a lot of support to change his demeanour. His dress was changed, his 'uniform', work on his body-language and how he radiated in the world.

A month later, another film was made of him walking over the same bridge in a crowd. A different group of young offenders were asked who they would target, and *none of them* picked this young man. He was no longer projecting 'victim' out to the world.

We think, don't we, that being at the top of the food chain, we are sophisticated and above the laws on the jungle. Wrong! The veneer of civility is sometimes very thin. You only need to experience a city mainline train station in the rush hour to see how quickly human beings revert to the laws of the jungle. It's every person for themselves, and woe betide you if you're too weak to fight.

If you watch a wildlife programme on TV, and see a big cat pick out their prey. They can be going after an animal much larger than them, but they wait and see which beast is the weak link in the chain, which one is the easy prey, the 'victim'.

Well, despite our intelligence, advances in technology and language etc. we are at heart all animals and it doesn't take much to revert to those deep-rooted instincts. I know it's horrid to think about and unpleasant to comprehend, but it's true. Best we're aware of the reality and ensure we don't put ourselves in the category of 'the weakest link'.

You are a powerhouse of authority and fabulousness, make sure you present yourself in a way that everyone else knows it too.

Now you have really started to acknowledge how great the body you were born with is, and you have an idea of what to do so you can celebrate that body with joy, let's track back in time and have a look at how our powerful emergence has been reflected by our clothes over the decades.

Onto the next chapter then.

Chapter Five
Your Wardrobe, Costume and Dress

'A woman is like a tea bag. She only knows her strength when put in hot water.'
Nancy Reagan

If we look back in history, the global and political changes have had a huge impact on women's dress or 'costume' and we can trace the advancement of women in the Western World easily by simply looking at what we wore. The more external power we have gained, the more our dress has mirrored that to the outside world.

The women leaders of our recent history were truly remarkable, not only for their achievements but in their abilities to not lose the essence of who they were. With my immediate history I can see this clearly with my female ancestors.

If we look back through the decades we can trace the journey.

1890 – 1909
Women of influence

Emmeline Pankhurst *– founder of National Women's Social and Political Union*

Marie Curie

Helena Rubenstein *– opened her first salon in 1908*

Lucile *– designer responsible for the invention of lingerie and the bra*

The suffragette movement, and their voice, was becoming louder during this time, we would have to wait a while before changes started to take shape, but women were waking up more and more to the issues and the need for change.

Women had a lot of matriarchal power at this time. The married woman was seen as having more authority and status, reflected by the greater choice available to those women. We wore our power on our heads, emphasising the hair style and drawing attention to our 'triangle of influence' with eye catching hats. The benchmark for Ladies Day at Ascot perhaps?

1910 – 1919
Women of influence

Lillian Gish

Mary Pickford – *she founded United Artists with D W Griffith, Charlie Chaplin and husband Douglas Fairbanks*

Gloria Swanson

Jeanne Lanvin – Designer

Elizabeth Arden – opened her first salon in 1910

This was the decade that saw the rise in the suffragette riots, it was also the decade dominated by the First World War which affected change for ever, particularly for women when their social liberation really started to take hold. With women taking on roles they otherwise had not had access to, the social mores of the western world were beginning to soften and merge, women had a much broader view of the world during this time, which inevitably translated into changes in their personal lives.

Newly-won independence was reflected in less opulent fashion, hair was shorter, initially for practicality, the Women's Land Army was started in 1917, we had an elevated waist with the Empire Line, sweaters and skirts as well as dresses.

1920 – 1929
Women of influence

Marie Stopes – *changed women's contraception and sexual health for ever*

Coco Chanel

Suzanne Lenglen – *Wimbledon Women's Champion for eight years*

Louise Brooks – *signature severe bob, Vidal Sassoon's inspiration perhaps?*

Madeleine Vionnet – *Designer who freed the body of the corset and still showed the female shape*

LEGS! We had them – and arms – wow! A major step forward for women. The age of the flapper, the charleston and the birth of jazz. This was an era of fun and frivolity, after the austerity and horror of the First World War, this was probably the first time in history that women really started to play with the men. It was one big world fiesta. We were gaining more freedom and independence, and we demonstrated this by showing off bare flesh, putting our make-up on in public (scandalous darling!) and smoking. With the release from the corset, we had freedom in every way. This was the decade that saw women fully recognising that beauty was a way to express their personality and power.

1930 – 1939
Women of influence

Nancy Astor – *the first woman to sit in the House of Commons*

Wallis Simpson

Greta Garbo – *the epitome of haughty chic*

Marlene Dietrich

Amelia Earhart

Amy Johnson

Forget the racy 1920s and enter the too cool for school 1930s. Curves were making a comeback, and women were experimenting with a masculine image (think Marlene Dietrich) high class, aloof, sex appeal was the look. Trousers featured largely in this decade – from silky PJs to tailored pants to sporty numbers. Clothes had movement and sophistication.

1940 – 1949
Women of influence

Ingrid Bergman

Bette Davis

Vera Lynn

Eleanor Roosevelt

Edith Piaf

The Women's Land Army was reformed and this translated into quite a military look for women in this decade. Pencil skirts were the key look, worn with boxy little jackets with epaulettes and pill-box hats. The strapless evening dress was the fashion statement to be seen in (requiring internal scaffolding to ensure a lack of wardrobe malfunction). Jeans and T Shirts made their first appearance. We really saw women doing a lot of 'men's work' here, expanding on the experiences during the First World War. Not only did we have the Women's Land Army but women signed up to the Armed Forces too, a major step forward.

1950 – 1959
Women of influence

Jacqueline Cochran – *first woman to break the sound barrier*

Rosa Parks – *USA, she refused to give up her seat to a white man on a bus, she was known as the mother of the Civil Rights Movement*

Audrey Hepburn

Elizabeth Taylor

Grace Kelly

We were back to fun and frivolity, but with a lot more influence than we'd ever had. This was the decade represented by Hollywood Glamour. The peroxide hair, the red lips, the pinched-in waists, the full skirts. Matriarchal power was back, but this time instead of hats, the Beehive took over, spontaneous evenings out, getting ready in a blink of eye, were definitely NOT part of this decade! We had rock and roll (very risqué) the Teddy Boys, skin-tight trousers (think Olivia Newton John in Grease). Women's bodies were changing, we were becoming more toned and curvy. With the arrival of labour-saving devices in the home we had more leisure time. There was a new phrase in town 'The Career Woman'. *Vogue* featured an article in 1950 on The Working Mother, a shocking concept at that time but really emphasised how women were advancing – and quickly.

1960 – 1969
Women of influence

Jackie Kennedy Onasis

Twiggy

Mary Quant

Vivienne Westwood

Elizabeth Kubler-Ross, *Swiss Psychiatrist*

Mother Theresa

The major turning point for women in this decade was the pill. For the first time we had real control of whether or not we got pregnant, and this translated into considerably more freedom in how we showed off our bodies. Showing more skin was now a real statement for women 'I'm in control'. We had the mini skirt, hot pants and (heaven help us) the baby doll. It was a decade of political confrontation – the people versus the establishments, with anti-war marches, women being at the forefront of these. Jeans, T-shirts and long hair, from the back it could be hard to figure out who was male and who was female!

1970 – 1979
Women of influence

Indira Ghandi

Golda Meir

Barbara Hulanicki – *BIBA*

Germaine Greer

Boy, did we mean business! 'Don't mess with us guys' was the emerging message in this decade.

We had (sadly) the boob tube and skin-tight lycra pants in unbelievable neon colours (I know because I wore them!). We also had punk – a huge anti-establishment movement, women were presenting themselves in a way they had never done before – aggressive, mean and intimidating. Not pleasant to look at, but it carried a powerful message and lay the foundations for women coming up behind them that being pushed around was no longer an option.

This was also the decade that saw the birth of the designer jean, keep fit really took off too, with dance centres opening up all over the place and Jane Fonda telling us to 'feel the burn'.

1980 – 1989
Women of influence

Margaret Thatcher

Nancy Reagan

Anita Roddick

Barbara McClintock – *US Scientist who won the Nobel Prize in 1983*

Oprah Winfrey

Love her or hate her Margaret Thatcher had a massive global impact for women.

We had *Dallas* and *Dynasty* launching shoulder pads into the world that would make most American footballers weep with envy, we had hair so rigid it wouldn't move in a force-ten gale and earrings that were offering potential lasting damage to our ear lobes. We were breaking into previously male-dominated working environments like never before – law, banking, stock-broking, the military, the trading floor. Our dress was very masculine at times – structured suits, tailored trousers, angular and masculine briefcases, the look was very hard and sharp – power dressing was born.

1990 – 1999
Women of influence

Madeleine Albright

Victoria Wood

Kate Moss and other supermodels

We had *Friends* on television, *The Spice Girls* and *Thelma and Louise* at the cinema.

Women living life their way, without compromise, calling the shots and making the rules. Freedom from the expectation of 'marrying and settling down'. Children were taking longer to arrive, singledom was 'in', the career was the new 'baby'.

We started to see far more choice in women's fashion during this decade, the power dressing was starting to decline, with authority dressing taking its place. And yes, there is a difference. Power dressing is what women did for themselves and was necessary at the time, as it was making a loud statement that needed to be heard. Authority dressing is what we do for other people and a way in which we communicate our essence, which is the way women naturally interact and carries far more influence long term.

This was the decade women started to have the opportunity to find their own style and create their own personal brand.

2000 – Present Day
Women of influence

Hilary Clinton

Angela Merkel

Karren Brady

Benazir Bhutto

Stella Rimmington

Femininity in dress is really back – but now it is translated in a confident and relaxed way. All the major changes have happened, we can relax more now and settle into our own 'brand' knowing that who we are will always be more powerful than trying to fit the mould of what's expected of us visually. We can show off our personal style and express our true selves. It's OK to be feminine and curvy, it's OK to be boyish and cheeky, it's OK to be angular and dramatic, it's OK to be youthful and perky, it's OK to be a tomboy and natural.

Anything goes really sums up where we are now. We've come a long way, let's not waste what we have, what women before us fought so hard to achieve. Let us honour them all by embracing our true freedom and expressing ourselves in a way that respects us, the people we interact with and all women – past, present and future – because we also have a responsibility to women following on behind us not to sabotage their choices.

What does this mean to you now?

It can be difficult to make sense of all the choice sometimes. It is easier isn't it to stick to an expected 'uniform'? If you ever had to wear a uniform at school, particularly secondary school, you will know that no choice can be less stressful than too much choice.

So it's really crucial in the times we are living in now to know your personal brand, be sure of who you are, what you represent to others, how you want to be seen and the mark you want to make on the world. Then ensure that your visual image is in alignment with all of them. Because if it isn't, as I've already mentioned, people will get confused, you will be giving off mixed messages that can have a detrimental impact on how you are viewed by others.

SOME THINGS TO THINK ABOUT

Budgeting

Not the most exciting word in the world I know. But just how much do you value your clothes and your wardrobe? If you don't place a high enough importance on the visual part of your personal brand, how can you expect other people to take you seriously? I don't mean everything has to be Designer labels or Couture, that's totally unrealistic, what I mean is, consider the impact your clothes have and ensure they are saying what you would like them to say about you.

So, how much do you spend on your visual impact every year? I'm talking about everything concerned with your visual impact here, not just clothes:

your hair
dry cleaning
facials
make-up
nails
shoes
accessories
gym membership

How much of your net annual income does that sum represent?

0%, 5%, 15%, 25%, 30% - more?

The figure you should be thinking about is between ten to fifteen per cent of your net income. Anything less and you're not putting yourself high enough up the list and anything considerably more and you're probably over doing it, it's important yes, but there is more to life.

Figure out what that sum is and then stick to it. If you are able to, at the start of every year put the money aside in a separate account. If you can't do that, ensure you keep track of money spent and how much is left of your annual budget.

If you do this, something wonderful happens – you can afford anything. And something else wonderful happens, if you can afford it you know whether or not you really want it. Budgeting makes you a much better decision maker, it also takes away the guilt (you know in the past you've sneaked something indoors and pretended you've had it for years).

Think about your capsule wardrobe – how can your clothes work hard for you and do the job you want them to do. This is a question I ask all my clients prior to a wardrobe session. Ask yourself – If I won the lottery this weekend, how much of this wardrobe would I keep?

Your own check list

Thinking of your personal brand and the impact you have, complete the table on the following page and consider how you are seen by colleagues, bosses and socially. You might want to be careful about 'on a par with everyone else' thinking that you're OK, as everyone else may have got it wrong.

The last one you may need to ask someone you trust who spends a lot of time looking at you or being around you, as we are rarely aware of any distracting habits that we might have, but other people will be very aware of them. They are things like – fiddling with rings if you're nervous, twiddling your hair, constantly shaking your foot when listening or in a meeting, playing with your pen, looking bored and showing your emotions too much on your face. All these will distract people from what you are saying as a professional woman and you want to avoid them at all costs if you can.

	An asset	On a par with everyone else	Needs development
Posture	☐	☐	☐
Body-language	☐	☐	☐
Smile and expression	☐	☐	☐
Handshake	☐	☐	☐
Eye-contact	☐	☐	☐
Use of voice	☐	☐	☐
Smart business wear	☐	☐	☐
Business casual wear	☐	☐	☐
Accessories	☐	☐	☐
Grooming	☐	☐	☐
Hairstyle and maintenance	☐	☐	☐
Listening skills	☐	☐	☐
Well-organised and tidy	☐	☐	☐
Enthusiasm and energy	☐	☐	☐
Fitness and stamina	☐	☐	☐
Absence of distracting habits	☐	☐	☐

So, we've reached the end of Part Two, Who Are You On The Outside. Now it's time for you to really get to grips with what might be holding you back, digging deep to flush out any limitations you might be inadvertently putting in your own way.

Time to find out who you are on the inside.

Part Three
Who Are You
On The Inside?

Chapter Six
What Makes You Tick?

'A positive attitude may not solve all your problems, but it will annoy enough people to make it worth the effort!'
Herm Albright

Have you any idea how magnificent you are?

OK, let's go right back to your conception. As we know it's quite a fight for the sperm to get to the egg, and thousands don't make it. The one that does make it is already a part of you, already has more strength and determination and spirit than the other thousands that fell by the wayside. You are already unique! You are special, talented and fabulous.

Women are far more likely to withdraw from shining, most women feel it is 'too pushy' to be out there promoting themselves, a bit 'cocky'. Most women believe they are frauds and are just waiting to be 'found out'. 'If I stay in the background, don't draw attention to myself, no-one will spot me and I can stay safe.' Sound familiar?

It's where I was for a long time in my life, certainly growing up, I wouldn't want to go back to my teenage years for any amount of money. They were full of confusion, self-doubt and self-consciousness. A lot of that I carried around with me for many years, and it had a huge impact on the decisions I made in my life, personal and professional. It took a lot of hard work and introspection to make the shift. But make it I did. Why did I bother to put myself through all that pain?

IF YOU DON'T SHINE – HOW CAN ANYONE ELSE?

So many people have so much invested in keeping people close to them exactly where they are in their life. Because if those people were to change, then that would show up their own 'inadequacies'. How many people do you know (personal and professional) who haven't been as supportive and pleased for you in a certain area as you thought they were going to be? Maybe you've lost a lot of weight and expected all your friends to be overjoyed and they weren't, maybe you've had a promotion at work and thought everyone in your team would celebrate your success and they didn't. It can come as quite a shock to realise that other people's fears will be projected onto us at times during our life. But remember, their reaction is everything to do with how they're feeling about themselves and absolutely nothing to do with how they're feeling about you. So many people feel threatened by others' success.

But the strong woman, the one everyone else will want to follow, the woman who is magnetic and charismatic, is the woman who is comfortable with who she is, happy to grow others underneath her, and joyful in celebrating the success of other people. Because once we 'know who we are' and are prepared to stick our head above the parapet and tell other people, what we do is open up the way for others to also shine, we give permission for those around us to grow and also become magnificent.

The wonderful Marianne Williamson poem, *Our Deepest Fear*, encapsulates this very message, I love it:

Our deepest fear is not that we are inadequate
Our deepest fear is that we are powerful beyond measure
It is our light, not our darkness that most frightens us
We ask ourselves,
Who am I to be brilliant, gorgeous, talented, fabulous?
Who are you NOT to be?
You're playing small doesn't serve the world
There is nothing enlightened about shrinking so that others
won't feel insecure around you.
You are born to shine, as children do
You are born to make manifest the glory that is within you

It is not in some of us, it is in everyone
As you allow your own light to shine
You instinctively give others permission to do the same
As you are liberated from your fear
So your presence automatically liberates others

So – what is your fear? What do you need to be liberated from? When have you shone and that light has impacted on other people, and as a result they have started to shine? This doesn't have to be exclusively in your work life, this can be in your private life.

Become that shining star – if not for you then for other people. You are an example to others whatever you do in life, it's impossible not to be. We set examples all day, every day by our actions and reactions. Make sure your example is one that people want to copy, be the magnet they need to allow themselves to shine. If you don't give yourself permission, how do you give permission to other people to be magnificent? You might try, but it will come across without sincerity or authenticity.

Values

In order to know ourselves well it's really important to be aware of our values in life. The code by which we live, what we would like to be known for.

Our values determine our motivation in life, why we do things. We can have two types of values – means values and end values. To give an example, if we hold our physical fitness and having a healthy body on our list of end values, then taking some form of exercise and being aware of what we eat is very likely to be on our list of means values.

So why is it crucial to be consciously aware of our own values? Well, if people don't live by them, or find themselves in a situation where it is hard to adhere to them, this is likely to cause stress and a feeling of being unbalanced. You may not be consciously aware of this, but it will have an impact on you. It may be that you find yourself experiencing more headaches than usual, feeling your patience and temper are shortened, you feel tired and lethargic. It all feels slightly 'etherial' you can't really put your finger on one particular thing that is causing you to feel this way, but you know something isn't 'quite right'.

Our values are so deeply embedded as part of a person's DNA that if they are not honoured – we WILL know. It's a case of learning to listen to your body. Someone told me years ago 'listen to you body while it's whispering, don't wait until it starts shouting'. Such good advice. If you don't honour your own values, then at some level this will be picked up by other people and you won't come across with the same level of authenticity. We've all seen people being interviewed in the news, and we know that what they are saying they don't really believe, their words are going against what they hold dear, and because we sense that imbalance, we trust them less.

Don't let that happen to you.

So let's start to give it a bit of thought.

What are your values – what is crucial to you about how you live your life?

....

....

....

....

....

....

....

What messages are people receiving from you about your values – what do you stand for?

....

....

....

....

....

How well are you communicating your values to other people? Score yourself between 1 - 10

1 = very badly   10 = exceptionally well   ☐

How well are you honouring and living by your values? Score yourself between 1 – 10

1 = very badly   10 = exceptionally well   ☐

Beliefs

So are these different to values? Surely they're the same aren't they? Actually there is a difference. Values are part of our character and the personality that we are born with, an innate part of our DNA. Beliefs are things that we 'acquire' as we go through life, the thoughts and ideas we pick up from external referencing. People can find themselves living by them, even though they may not, actually, fit in with their values.

So which one has the most influence over us? That is individual to each person and can change as we go through life. Beliefs can come from a variety of sources:

Culture
Religion
Our parents
Our background
Our socio/economic status
Our desire to 'fit in' with those around us
What we think of ourselves

When we arrive on this planet as a new born, we haven't yet acquired any beliefs. Our values are there, but at this stage we are unaware of them. Our only aims at this point are to be fed, kept clean and loved.

As people go through their lives, they 'pick up' the beliefs of other people and absorb these, so they eventually become part of that person's belief-system. For a while the beliefs that are projected onto us may well be stronger than our values. The first people who are likely to instil a set of beliefs with us are, obviously, our parents. When we are young we, of course, aren't in a position to question the 'big people', so it's hardly surprising that the beliefs we are given during our formative years are those that we accept to be our truth.

Many people will grow up to vote in the same way as their parents did, 'believing' that of course, that particular party is the only one to support. If people are brought up in different socio/economic environment, that can have a huge impact on their belief-system. Many people who have experienced living within the benefit system as a child, because that was their 'truth', believe that they are not able to get out that and live another way. Religion and culture play a huge part in our belief-system, they are both extremely powerful in forming how we view the world, and therefore our actions and reactions, and ultimately what we believe we can and cannot achieve.

All of the above are a form of control over us, sometimes intentionally and sometimes unintentionally, but the result is likely to be the same. If we have been brought up and experienced a certain way of living and interacting with the world, it takes a very strong person to break that mould and live their own life, their way.

But this is what you need to do to become great. Never accept the status quo, always question the way things are done, and be very sure that the beliefs that impact on you and the way you live your life are the beliefs that *belong to you.* If you think your beliefs are non-nego-tiable and cannot be changed – according to whom exactly? It can take courage to go against the grain, to be a maverick in your own environment, to take a stand and be different. But if you *don't* live by your rules and your beliefs, you run the risk of looking back on your life later on and thinking 'If only', 'What a difference it would have made to my life if I had only had the courage'. Well, don't let that happen, now is your chance to really think about your beliefs, how you live your life, where those thought patterns have come from and which ones you want to keep and which ones need to be put out with the garbage.

As human beings, we really hate to be proved wrong. So we uncon-sciously go through life looking for the evidence to prove that we are right.

THERE ARE TWO KINDS OF PEOPLE IN THE WORLD, THOSE WHO THINK THEY CAN, AND THOSE WHO THINK THEY CAN'T. THEY'RE BOTH RIGHT!

If you have a belief that you can achieve something, then you will automatically look for ways of doing so, for the opportunities that will make it happen. This will have an impact on your capabilities, which in turn will give you new behaviours. These behaviours (be-liefs about ourselves) will impact on our environment and the way people react to us. What we give out, we get back, but we're likely to have that exaggerated about ten times.

If, on the other hand, you believe you can't achieve something, then you probably won't even look for opportunities, or if they present themselves to you, you won't recognise them as opportunities. This is likely to restrict your capabilities, your behaviour and your envi-ronment, which changes how people react to you.

72

Also, be very careful what you think and 'believe' about other people, as this can have an impact on their behaviour. If you believe someone is 'difficult', you will automatically be looking for the evidence to prove you are right, you will not see all the examples of when that person really works well with you and is 'on side'. The result may be that that person eventually starts to 'believe' that they are difficult, and then presents that evidence to you on a regular basis. Be very aware of what you are projecting onto people – you are likely to get it back squarely between the eyes with knobs on!

Start to challenge any limiting beliefs

Examples

I need to conform to the 'norm', have a steady job, get married (settle down) and fulfil the expectations of people around me

I haven't got the courage to be self-employed or go for that promotion

There's no way I could stand up in front of a group of people and give a talk

Other people lose weight/have great relationships/get great jobs – but that never happens to me

I'd love to go travelling, but could never do that on my own

I'd really like to go and talk to that person, but I have nothing interesting to say

When I have enough money, then I'll be 'happy'

Think about a belief you hold about yourself that may be limiting you in some way

....

....

....

....

What are the consequences of holding this belief?	

How does it cause you to behave?	

What evidence do you have to support this belief?	

In what way might this belief be ridiculous or absurd?	

Do you have examples in your life when this belief has been disproved?	

What caused you to have the belief in the first place, and do these assumptions still apply?	

Do you want to change the belief?	

If YES, what would be a better belief?	

Hold this new belief as though it were true for at least a week and notice:

• How your behaviour changes

• How other people's behaviour changes

To help you embed and develop a new empowering belief about yourself, find as many reasons, with as much evidence as possible to support it. Ask yourself when you have known this belief to be true for you.

Let's start you on the road to putting the rules in place that empower, inspire and help you throughout your life:

I CAN DO ANYTHING I SET MY MIND TO

The following exercises may not be easy, but they're here to help you really start to dig deep and expose some of the 'rubbish' that has been deep-rooted for far too long and may be getting in the way of you stepping into your true magnificence.

What do you believe you can do? (personally, professionally, financially, socially)

....

....

....

....

....

....

What do you believe you cannot do (personally, professionally, financially, socially)

....

....

....

....

....

Which one do you think has the most influence over you and why?

....

....

....

....

....

To what extent do you see yourself as having the necessary ability and confidence to succeed?

....

....

....

....

....

Some examples of enabling beliefs

There is always a way

I can do anything I set my mind to

There is no failure, only feedback

I have all the confidence within me that I need

Everybody is different and I respect his or her views and opinions

There is a solution to every problem

Everything happens for a reason – even if the reason isn't obvious at the time

An optimist is wrong just about as often as a pessimist but the BIG difference is that the optimist has a lot more fun!

I now want to challenge you on a belief I have found to be very high up the list with a lot of women I work with: 'I have to put everyone else higher up the list of importance than myself.'

Women are brilliantly talented at putting everyone else considerably higher up the 'importance' ladder than themselves. Women tell me 'I hate being selfish and always want to think of others before me, it's how I operate and what I'm known for, everyone relies on me'.

Fabulous.

But who do YOU rely on?

Do you want to be selfish or selfless? I want to challenge you on your perception of being 'selfish' and 'selfless'.

I'm going to use the analogy of flying.

So, you're strapped in, overhead lockers have all been closed, the plane's taxiing and getting ready to find its slot in the take off schedule. The cabin crew then take you through the safety procedures.

You remember the bit where they tell us 'should the plane loose pressure, an oxygen mask will fall down from above you, before helping those around you, ensure you attach your own mask first'. You know what? They say that for a reason. In that situation and in all other situations in life, if we don't look after ourselves first we are in a very poor place to help anyone else. Imagine your body is a bottle full of energising liquid (champagne always works for me). If that bottle becomes depleted of resources, and what's left is then given to other people, the people you are wanting to support and help are never getting the best of you and what they do get is likely to be given with an element of resentment – which is *selfish*.

However, if you ensure that your bottle of energy is always topped up and overflowing – ie you look after yourself well then what other people are getting is the very best of you, which you give with love and willingly – this is *selfless*.

If you don't value yourself how can you expect anyone else to?

If you're not prepared to take good care of 'you' why should anyone else bother?

If you don't think you're worth it – guess what? No-one else will either.

YOU ARE YOUR MOST PRECIOUS ASSET – MAKE SURE YOU CHERISH THAT ASSET, NURTURE IT, LOVE IT AND ALLOW IT TO GROW AND BLOSSOM.

Start developing positive beliefs.

These will keep you within an upward cycle of good self-esteem in your private and professional life.

I can't expect everyone to like me – after all, I don't like everyone I meet

I have strengths to offer if I choose

I have achieved some positive things in my life and I will again

I have a right to think differently and believe in different things than other people

I have got all sorts of interesting ideas and experiences that I can share if I want to

Making mistakes is OK – I can learn from these – and it allows others to as well

I can understand and forgive other people who have hurt me, being 'adult' means that I can start to sort things out for myself; I don't have to go on blaming people

Sometimes new experiences are very exciting

I can't solve all the problems I'm confronted with – sometimes I might have to choose to live with them or remove them or myself from them

I have dreams and hopes that make me special and unique

I have had some good relationships in the past and I will again in the future

I am not an endless 'resource' for others, I must stock up on 'reserves' and not get too drained

I have inner creative talents which have been hidden for a long time and need a chance to grow

The 'perfect' partner, boss, colleague, child does not exist – the 'good enough' one does!

I don't have to have everyone's approval all the time to know that I'm trying my hardest

I owe it to myself and those in my life to always believe in myself

Now select one that you need to believe in more strongly and write it down where you can see it every day – read it and believe it.

Your internal dialogue.

We all have internal messages in our heads, and when we wake up in the morning we hit the 'start' button and when we go to sleep at night we hit the 'end' button. Are your recordings positive or negative? Have you any idea what you say when you talk to yourself?

Some women I work with have negative messages which get replayed on a regular and frequent basis. These can be anything from:

'Oh for goodness sake, I knew I'd forget to get that jacket cleaned.'

'I don't believe it, I've burnt the toast AGAIN, what an idiot!'

'Where did I put the keys, why don't I remember to put them in the same place?'

To rather more serious ones:

'There's no way I'm good enough to get that job, so there's no point applying for it.'

'Why am I so fat/ugly/unstylish/frumpy/thin/young/old?' (delete as appropriate)

'I'll never be as good X, so why bother?'

'Success is for other people, if I go for it, I'll only be 'found out' eventually.'

The rather worrying thing is, your mind cannot tell the difference between truth and lies, therefore it will assume that everything you tell it is your truth, and as it wants to please you, it will work very hard at making that 'truth' become your reality. So when you tell your mind 'I'm rubbish' your mind will rub its hands together and say 'fabulous, how can we work as a team to make that happen in your life then?'.

> BE VERY CAREFUL WHAT YOU SAY TO YOURSELF
> AS SELF-FULFILLING PROPHECIES ARE
> FRIGHTENINGLY EASY TO ACHIEVE.

You may well be thinking, 'What's the difference between beliefs and internal messages?'. On the surface, they appear to be the same thing, but there is a distinct difference. It's actually your beliefs that will create your messages. Beliefs are very deep and well hidden and we are rarely consciously aware that they exist, yet they dictate strongly how we live. Internal messages, on the other hand, are on the surface and use our heads as a gymnasium, swinging from the ropes and trampolining to the forefront of our thoughts all the time.

Some of my old recordings and messages.

I wore glasses from the age of ten, and was picked on at school remorselessly as a result, one of the 'sound tracks' of my early teenage years was 'boys never make passes at girls in glasses'. So I never wore them when I went out at the weekend, most of my teenage years were spent in a bit of a blur. Eventually I had to wear them, and realised that actually that message wasn't true – boys did make passes at girls in glasses, and for the first time I could actually see them. But I had a recording for years that I would never have a boyfriend because my glasses made me ugly and was hugely self-conscious as a teenager as a result. That message stayed with me for years, I did get contact lenses and struggled with those for a couple of decades, I now have daily disposals and alternate between glasses and lenses, I now feel really fabulous in my glasses, but it took a rewriting of my internal messages to get me there.

I was in the first year of my secondary school and I loved English, unfortunately our English teacher for some reason appeared not to like me. I remember that one week we were writing an essay on a particular subject, I was sitting at the back of the class and the girl sitting next to me leant over and copied me. I wasn't brave enough to confront her, so said nothing. I was really proud of my essay and was looking forward to getting it back the following week and seeing my mark. What I got was an 'F' with the written comment 'Don't try and copy Olivia, Katie, you'll never be as good as she is'. The absolute injustice of that stayed with me for years and years. I started to believe that I wasn't any good at English, which impacted hugely on my school learning and my choices when I left school, and left me with the internal message, 'I'm not as good as others'.

There have been others, but I won't bore you too much, you get the picture. I don't hold these or any other negative messages any more, I recognise that they are, in fact, fantasy and not part of my past, current or future reality.

Yes, I still talk to myself, we all do and it's impossible to stop that, but now my inner talk is positive, I don't 'beat myself up' if I make a mistake, I try and use the experience to learn and grow. Sometimes a gremlin creeps in unannounced and uninvited, I'm only human. But because I'm consciously aware of them now, I can deal with the negative quickly and efficiently. I look at it, decide if there is any truth in it at all, and if there is, learn from it and then immediately delete it.

Do you know what you say when you talk to yourself? Have you ever been consciously aware of these messages that you give your 'self' and are in danger of believing?

Try not to define yourself by the messages you give yourself, or other people hang on you. At a workshop I was running recently there was a fabulous, inspiring, funny, upbeat and amazing woman attending. She told us all she was 'an angry person' and wanted to address that. People had told her that she had 'anger issues', and she had defined herself by that belief.

I really want to challenge any similar beliefs you may be holding about yourself, any messages you regularly replay internally. Recognise that we all experience emotions, that's part of being human, they keep us safe, allow us to make appropriate decisions and help us grow. It is wrong, however, to stay stuck in one emotion and believe that is 'who you are'. Anger is there to help you recognise what is, and is not, right for you in life. Which action, treatment, situations are supportive of you and which are potentially holding you back. Anger is not, however, who you *are*. Recognise that emotions are there to assist you and support you.

When they show up, bring them out of your conscious mind and bring them to in front of your eyes, disengage them from your 'self', and look at them. Ask yourself the following questions:

How appropriate is this emotion to the situation?

Have I got this emotion in balance?

How can this emotion help me?

When should I let it go?

Then thank the emotion for turning up and, when appropriate, send it on its way. Emotions are not 'you'. They are there to give us a helping hand when we need them, but they do not define who we are in the world. Please don't allow other people to stigmatise you with a label. It's their 'stuff' they are dealing with at this point, and they have no right to dump it on you.

Start to become aware of that internal iPod, which messages are supportive of you and which really need to be deleted pronto. Can you identify where they came from? Usually a throw-away comment from our childhood can trigger all sorts of 'beliefs' about ourselves as we grow up. The trouble is, when we're knee high to a grasshopper we're not in a position to challenge these messages. As a small person we automatically assume that everything the big people tell us is true, the trust of a child is total. So with each message we receive, the one before it gets stuffed down a little further, and gradually becomes more embedded, and eventually a part of how we live and the decisions we make.

Some potential throw-away comments you may have had said to you, or heard said to others:

Could try harder (end of term report at school)

Never concentrates – probably won't amount to much (as above)

Never mind, you're not as pretty as your sister, but at least

you have your brain (any family member)

Thank goodness you're pretty, as your sister has all the brains of the family! (as above)

Money doesn't grow on trees – there's not enough to go round (I'll come to that one later in the book and start to challenge your thinking on abundance)

You're stupid

You're ugly/fat/thin

Identify some of your own recordings and messages

....

....

....

....

Where have these come from?

....

....

....

....

How can you change a negative message into a positive one, or at least neutralise it?

....

....

....

Challenging your negative self-talk.

To what extent do you really believe in yourself? If you truly see yourself as a successful person with the ability and confidence to succeed, you are far more likely to do just that – succeed. When your self-image is in line with your vision for your future, your future will be achieved more quickly, with more joy and considerably less stress.

Some women do have a poor self-image and opinion of themselves, and are far more likely to beat themselves up than pat themselves on the back. An opportunity to pat yourself on the back is coming in the next chapter – I want you to spend a little time getting rid of negativity first. A poor self-image is usually reinforced daily by those internal messages:

I'm no good at...

I'm hopeless at...

I can't do...

I'm useless at...

I'm awful at ...

This continual negative self-talk will eventually turn into a limiting belief. When considering your own self-talk earlier, what could you replace the negative messages with? You do have a choice in how you respond to key events or situations.

If you find yourself saying any of the messages on the following page to yourself on a regular basis, then you run the risk that these become your beliefs and will keep you in a negative cycle in your personal and professional life.

I've never been any good at…

I need lots of approval to know I'm doing the right thing

I've got to show that I'm capable all the time in order for people to like me and or me to like myself

If things go wrong or I make a mistake then life is terrible and I'm completely miserable

Nice people continuously do things for other people and put their needs first

I must show I'm in control of my emotions, 'letting go' is a sign of weakness

It's too late to change as I've always been like this

It's important that I keep my life and other lives as easy and even as possible, if I changed it could disrupt everything too much and people won't like me

If someone is negative towards me it must be my fault in some way

Remember – positive-thinking leads to positive results which leads to positive self-esteem

Staying Motivated

This is all very well in theory, of course. All these positive affirmations and turning negative into positive messages, telling yourself every day you're fantastic before you leave the house. Sounds wonderful, but then real life kicks in.

The alarm didn't go off and you're running late.

The children are ill and the whole schedule for the day is suddenly out of the window.

A few niggles with the other half have left you feeling negative.

It's a *really* bad-hair day frankly and *nothing* is going to make it any better.

You're tired, stressed and to be honest, right now actually couldn't give a ****!

First things first – breathe! It's amazing that when stress and negativity creeps up on us, the most fundamental things in life go AWOL and we forget to breathe. And by breathing I mean breathing correctly, not the little shallow breaths we all do every day (more about the right breathing later in the book when I talk about having a strong voice).

Life isn't perfect, bad stuff happens, always has, always will. It's how we deal with it that matters. We can choose to let the negative take us over and dictate how the rest of that day unfolds or we can choose to rise above it and move on, recognising that the moment is only temporary and does not define who we are for that day.

How are you going to keep yourself motivated to remain positive if you come up against challenges?

Identify what potential challenges might arise in the future

....

....

....

....

What action can you take to overcome these challenges and remain positive?

....

....

....

What action can you take NOW to motivate yourself to achieve the future you want?

....

....

....

....

....

....

....

....

....

....

Positive Feedback

As I've alluded to earlier, our negative internal messages are, actually, fantasy and bear no relation to who we really are. Quite often other people will see us in a completely different way, their experience of us is personal to where they are on a particular day, or what part of their life's journey they are at.

Start to think about the people you know, both in your personal and professional life, both present and past, and then ask yourself the following questions:

Who have you helped?

Who loves you?

Who would miss you if you weren't around?

What knowledge do you have that others don't?

What experience do you possess that others could benefit from?

What do people say to you about what you mean to them?

When was the last time you laughed so much you thought you were going to be sick – who were you with?

Ask someone you trust and like (personal life or work life) to give you some feedback on YOU. Ask them for a positive character reference:

What do they admire about you?

What do they really appreciate about you?

If they were describing you to someone else, what would they say?

On a scale of 1 – 10, how much would they miss you if you weren't around?

Are you squirming yet?

Hard isn't it? Most people find this very difficult to do, but I'm leading you into the next chapter where I want you to GO FOR IT! I want you to start blowing your own trumpet and being proud of who you are.

These same people are perfect to help you change any negative messages into positive ones, so if you're willing to share your inner thoughts, ask for support and help.

Your Positive Feedback, capture what people have said about you, when asked, in the table on the following page.

Name	What they said about me

YOUR POSITIVE POWERFUL STATEMENT

Did you do the last exercise? If you did, how great did that feel? We have no idea what other people are thinking about us, or how much we mean to them, what we've done for them, how we've helped or inspired them. I told you that you were fabulous!

For the last part of this chapter, I'd really like you to take all the great feedback you've got from other people and come up with your own Powerful Statement that you take ownership of and really believe.

MY POSITIVE POWERFUL STATEMENT

If you can, put this somewhere where you can see it every day and read it to yourself regularly, first thing in the morning is a good idea as it creates a great way to start the day.

MY POSITIVE POWERFUL STATEMENT

Now that you have spent time really getting into those mind recesses and exposing the grime lurking behind strategically placed conscious thoughts, in the next Chapter I want you to begin to get in touch with your fabulousness, your very core and essence of wonder.

Chapter Seven
Become A Star And Be Proud

'Every life is a story, makes yours a best seller.'
Anonymous

YOUR SKILLS AND TALENTS

In the last chapter I talked about your values and beliefs, what the differences were between them and how important it is to live by your values. Also I started to ask you to look at your internal iPod and how it may be blocking you in some areas of your life.

Now I want you to start appreciating who you are – every aspect of who you are, not simply the person on your business card. Bearing in mind that title only represents an aspect of you and your life, and one that is transitory anyway. Next year you may have another title on your business card so don't plan your current life around that one small percentage of the total.

What I would like you to start doing is to fully celebrate you as a WHOLE, the essence of who you are, what makes you tick, all the amazing things you have already accomplished in however many years you've been around so far. We do tend to take ourselves for granted, men and women, but particularly women. Generally speaking women do find it harder to promote themselves and 'sell' themselves out there in the world, and may well fall into the trap of down-sizing their skills and talents so as not to appear cocky or arrogant. But as I've said earlier in the book, if you don't believe in yourself how can you expect other people to believe in you.

So this is your chance to really show off. This can be for your eyes only so don't get embarrassed. I want you to go back to your very first memory. What can you remember? When did you learn to ride a bike (I never progressed past a tricycle by the way, so not everyone can ride a bike!) When did you/can you:

First get a 'star' for a piece of school work?

Learn to drive?

Pass exams?

Go on holiday without parents or on your own?

Get your first job?

Experience your first public speaking experience?

Speak any languages fluently other than your mother tongue?

Cook brilliantly?

Achieve anything off the wall or amazing?

I've had some amazing examples here when
I do this with groups:

Hang-gliding

Parachuting/hot-air ballooning

White-water rafting

Trekking

Mountain climbing

Car racing

Running marathons

Putting on huge events

Raising money for charity

Volunteering in local communities

Maybe you've lived abroad and had to conquer all kinds of hurdles to survive and prosper, perhaps you're doing that now, living and working in the UK or elsewhere from another country and culture. Perhaps you've had very challenging financial times in your life and have survived and flourished despite adverse circumstances. Possibly you've successfully extricated yourself from a damaging personal relationship because you realised you deserved better and have rebuilt your life and confidence.

Whatever it is that is personal and special to YOU, I'd like you to capture now. Really dig deep within the recesses of your memory, nothing is too small to capture and remember. Also think about what qualities you possess that enables/enabled you to be that person. If you're a wonderful friend and partner – why? What is it about you that makes you a wonderful friend, is it your listening skills, nurturing nature, compassion, sense of fun and joy, being a brilliant organiser. Really get to the heart of who you are, all your fabulous bits! Get a notebook and use a whole page, even more if you can. Use colour so it's really visible and out there, don't hold back, remember no-one else need see this.

So what did that feel like? Did you feel a bit silly or did you really get into it and enjoy the experience? Whatever your personal experience, it is right for you right now, our views of the world are completely personal and we all experience what we need to at any given time.

Go back to this exercise whenever you feel like it. Maybe get a large A3, or bigger, sheet of paper and really go for it. Create your own vision of your magnificence, use pictures and images that capture the essence of who you are. Whenever you feel down, this is a great booster for the soul and energy.

Just think about what you have already achieved. You arrived on this planet completely empty and unable to do anything other than cry and make a mess! You've mastered walking, talking, reading and writing from that totally vulnerable and disempowered state for goodness sake, without taking into account everything else you've achieved – just think what else is stretching out in front of you to grab, become brilliant at, shine with.

Now I'd like you to be very specific and make a list, you've just done the random right brain activity, now it's time for the logical left brain activity. More about the differences of our brain, and how to get the differences to work for you, later in the book.

Following are a couple of exercises I'd like you to think about and complete, covering your personal and business life. Ten is just a guide, you don't have to come up with ten in each section, but I would strongly advise you to try to. You can, of course, have more, whatever feels right.

My skill set – A personal view

What are your attributes, skills, knowledge or qualities? My skills are:

1 ....

2 ....

3 ....

4 ....

5 ....

6 ....

7 ....

8 ....

9 ....

10 ....

My skill set – An employer's view

If I was an employer, the things I would hire myself to deliver specifically would be:

1 ....

2 ....

3 ....

4 ....

5 ....

6 ....

7 ....

8 ....

9 ....

10 ....

Assets and Liabilities

What do I mean by that exactly? Well we all have 'assets and liabilities' – good bits and bad bits about ourselves. Or at least that is what we believe to be true about ourselves, usually because that is what someone else has told us. I'm linking back to those internal messages, and the fact that what we believe about ourselves may have come from someone else's view of the world.

It is really important to know your assets and liabilities. This allows you to raise your confidence, to make the right goals for you and be aware of manageable time scales and allow you to know of any situations which may create challenges or produce easy success. Your assets are also the way in which you can tangibly show your values to the world. Your values will always underpin your assets and dictate your behaviour, it is therefore crucial to keep assets in balance so that you continuously celebrate and honour your values.

I'd like you to start capturing your current view of your own assets and liabilities in the table on this and the next page.

List your assets – the things about you that you feel are positive, then do the same for your perceived liabilities.

Your assets	Your liabilities

Now that you've done that, I'd really like to challenge you on what you have written in the liabilities box. Because, in fact, there are no such things as liabilities! Whatever you have just written in the above box are simply your character strengths that are temporarily out of balance.

What do I mean by that? Well, a character strength becomes an asset when it is the appropriate reaction for the situation and benefits you and other people. A character strength becomes a liability when it goes to the extreme in either direction.

For example, being open and friendly with people is a wonderful, warm character strength. But if someone went too far with that personality trait, they could become overpowering and intrusive without a clear idea of boundaries, if they took it too far in the other direction, they may become insular, closed and people could feel awkward around them.

So what I'd like you to do now is to look back at the list of your perceived 'liabilities' and decide what character strength is underlying them, that you may currently have out of balance.

Capture your thoughts here:

....

....

....

....

....

....

....

....

....

....

....

....

Some of these examples may get you going:

Liability

Controlling – of yourself and other people
• *Character strength* – the ability to get things done, focussed and disciplined

• *Be aware of* - not taking over all the time, letting go of your possible fear of what may happen if you relinquish control

Always helping other people – being the one everyone else comes to

• *Character strength* – a wonderful, warm personality that invites people into your space

• *Be aware of* – not looking after yourself sufficiently (remember the oxygen in the plane example), becoming overpowering with your help and disempowering other people

Lazy – physical activity, work loads, life generally

• *Character strength* – the ability to not let life get on top of you, to be able to take life as it comes and not suffer with stress

• *Be aware of* – too much lethargy as it will encourage stagnation rather than growth, do not let life pass you by

Sometimes it can be really very hard to pinpoint the character strength underpinning the perceived liability. When we do something routinely and often, it very quickly becomes a part of who we are therefore tricky to separate from our 'being' and difficult to look at objectively.

Many times when running courses I get women who get stuck at this point, they may have put down 'Can't say no' in their liabilities but can't find the character strength there. The personality trait that underpins their character is a fabulous gift of being there for people, being a great team-player and supportive of others. It has just been taken to an extreme to the detriment of the person concerned and needs to be brought back into balance so that everyone benefits. If that character strength was taken to the other extreme, then the person would likely become rigid and tunnel visioned, not able to help or assist anyone which would eventually alienate them from others.

I also get examples of absolute specifics rather than personal qualities, for example 'I'm hopeless at maths and budgeting'. This in itself isn't a personal quality that is out of balance, more a perceived lack in someone's ability to perform certain tasks. If something like that crops up in your list, really look at it. Where did that 'internal message' come from that you're not very good at something? Is it really true or something that has been projected onto you by others? If it is true, that's fine too. We can't be brilliant at everything and accepting that empowers us to find ways round those tasks without guilt. Could I do my Tax Return every year? Probably, if I really put my mind to it. Do I want to? Not in a million years, it bores the pants off me! So the very first thing I outsourced as soon as my company could afford it all those years ago was an excellent bookkeeper and accountant. That's now one less thing for me to worry about.

Once you have identified your character strengths and become aware of when you may take them to extremes, you are perfectly placed to know what action, if any, you need to take to ensure you maintain the equilibrium in your life.

Now I'd like you to capture all your character strengths, and create a tangible version of your values and personality traits, that are in addition to those you have just discovered.

My character strengths are:

....

....

....

An example of using them well is:

....

....

....

Think back to comments from other people in your life – either at work or in your personal life. What throw-away comments have you heard about yourself that you may have ignored or paid little attention to. These could have been really positive affirmations of how people value you.

In addition, other people say I am good at:

....

....

....

....

Feeling good? I hope so. It's great to really get in touch with everything you've achieved, all your good points. But let's make absolutely sure that you really have got rid of gremlins that have been lurking for a long time and getting in your way. Let's spend a bit of time in the next chapter digging even deeper, and banishing anything hiding in a corner of your unconscious so you can fully liberate yourself.

Chapter Eight
How To Get Out Of Your Own Way

'You have to be the change you want to see.'
Ghandi

The thing that stops most women really pushing themselves forward to be great in the world is their own belief about themselves. Generally speaking, women don't promote themselves as well or effectively as men, I've already touched on this point. No-one knows you're out there if you don't get out there and tell them. Women are their own worst enemy and will get in their own way far more than anyone else will. So in this chapter I want to challenge you on how you have viewed yourself up to this point, who are you keeping yourself back for, what have you got invested in becoming stagnant, to help you identify your blocks and give you skills to overcome these and clearly see the path ahead. I'm not saying there will be no obstacles in the future, but at least you'll have strategies to deal with them should they show up.

The 'Poor Me' Syndrome

If you suffer from this in any area of your life, you really need to break it. It is one of the most debilitating and soul-destroying mind-sets anyone can carry with them through life. Unfortunately it's also one of the easiest to fall into.

What I've noticed a lot with my work over the years is the general 'lack' mentality that we live with and how easy it is for people, and again particularly women, to bond over bad news. There is a lot of comfort in being part of the gang of women who put themselves down, that common thread of disenchantment that can pull down fabulous women and keep them disempowered. There has been so much practice of 'lack' during our lives that it is so much easier to 'join the club'. Lack of: money, opportunities, time, energy, enthusiasm, jobs, men, support.

If you recognise yourself here, I want to challenge you to snap out of this mind-set. It is stopping you from being amazing every day, achieving what you are capable of, and giving yourself permission to shine and live your life's purpose.

Have you ever done something that has taken other people out of their comfort zones? You may have lost a lot of weight for example, achieved a wonderful promotion at work because (heaven forbid) you believed in yourself and went for it, even had a new haircut and colour and bought a new set of amazing clothes? Was everyone's re-action what you were expecting? Did everyone celebrate your wins and success? Or did one or two (or maybe more) people, who you were expecting to be really happy for you, actually try and put you down, or were clearly very *unhappy* for you? Bit of a shock isn't it?

What happens when we go out there and do something that breaks the mould is that we highlight to other people their own inadequa-cies. Because deep down, they know that they, too, could achieve and do similar things if they only got off their backsides, believed in themselves a little more and gave it a go. When we change we actu-ally have to support other people through our own process. People can feel threatened by us and have a lot invested in keeping us exactly where we are. Sometimes pushing against that can be very hard and it's a lot easier to just capitulate and stay bonded in the negativity. But you know what? That doesn't help anyone, you or them.

Remember the Marianne Williamson poem earlier in the book?

'If we allow our own light to shine, we instinctively give others permission to do the same,
If we become liberated from our fear, then our presence automatically liberates others.'

If we can support others through our change process, then we are giving them permission to change too and liberating them from their own blocks.

Staying where you are or moving forward

Let's look at where you are now and where you'd like to be. Just take stock and tune in to yourself – where are you in your life right now? Are you where you would like to be, has your life gone to plan? And just ask yourself – who's plan is it, yours or someone else's? Go back to when you were a child, while you were growing up did anyone ask you what you wanted to do when you left school/education? What was your answer? Where did you see yourself at this stage in your life? If you're not where you thought you'd be, what got in the way, where were the obstacles and how did you overcome them, or did you NOT overcome them and you changed direction?

Just sit quietly and really listen to your body, it will tell you everything you need to know.

Try and be somewhere where there are no distractions or interruptions, take a few deep breaths (in through the nose and out through the mouth) and close your eyes if it helps you focus. Then think about where you are in your life at the moment, what's happening in your personal and business life. Then tune into your body and scan from top to bottom. Do you feel anything, are there any tensions or stresses anywhere in your body? If you think about your personal life where do you feel that? Maybe a fluttering in the tummy, a beat of your heart, a tension in your head, then do the same thinking about your business life, what are you feeling and where? Really *feel* what's working for you right now and what needs adjusting or changing altogether. Start to recognise when your body is telling you when something feels right and when something feels wrong and get in touch with your intuition. Women are brilliant at gut reactions and inner knowing and if you can learn to trust this skill it will teach you all you need to know.

When you're clear about what's working really well, make a note of it opposite, and similarly when you're clear about what's not working well, make a note of that too.

What's working well in my life

....

....

....

....

....

What's NOT working well in my life

....

....

....

....

....

When you've identified what's working well, see if you can capture those things outside of this book and have them somewhere where you can see them every day or take them with you. When you're feeling down these are a great way to give you a boost.

What I'd like you to concentrate on now is what's not working well in your life, and I want you to ask yourself the following questions:

What have I got invested in staying exactly where I am?
Who do I not want to upset?
Who am I trying to please?
What am I scared of if I make changes?
Do I want to break the chain of past experiences?

What are your answers? Capture anything that comes into your mind here:

....

....

....

What do other people have invested in keeping you where you are?

Who are these people if they exist? Parents? Partner? Friends? Colleagues? Children? Anyone else?

....

....

....

What are they frightened of? What haven't they achieved that they wish they had? Think about how you can support them through your change process and make it safe for them for you to grow and be who you are really meant to be. Know deep within yourself that any jealousy, resentment, lack of support or anger from anyone else is them telling you how they feel about themselves, NOT how they feel about you. So how can you make them feel better about themselves, what support do they need from you, can you take them with you on the journey?

Is there, in fact, anyone that you simply need to walk away from? I know this is a strong statement but it is human nature, particularly with women, to stick around out of duty/commitment/feeling guilty etc. This is your time to shine, no-one has the right to keep you down, you don't 'belong' to anyone, only yourself. True love is letting people go to be who they are meant to be, not keeping them tied down out of fear.

Remember the poem

'There is nothing enlightened about shrinking so that other
people won't feel insecure around you, you are born to shine.'

Moving forward

Let's start planning where you want to be.

Imagine you have just moved house and you've inherited a garden.
You have nothing invested in the garden, no emotional attachment
to anything in it, so you can be completely objective and keep what
you like and get rid of what you don't.

Think of your life currently as that garden. If it helps, draw it out on
some paper. What does it look like? Where are the beautiful flowers,
fabulous bushes, gorgeous lawn, wonderful water features? Where
are the weeds, what's dying and needs pulling out or pruning? Be
ruthless, get rid of anything that doesn't work, anything that may be
clogging up the growth of something beautiful, anything that is dying and creating stagnation anywhere. Then draw how you would
like the garden to look, what are you going to plant and where?
What creates instant beauty and what will take time to grow and
flourish, where do you need to water the most and spend the most
time and attention, what parts of the garden will look after themselves with minimum effort by you? How will the garden look in six
months, twelve months, eighteen months, twenty four months, sixty
months? What parts of the upkeep do you need to do and which
bits can you delegate to others? Does it give you joy when you look
at your garden or does it feel like too much hard work? If it's the lat-
ter, where do you need to fine tune to create the joy within you?

Now you have an idea of how you would like your life to look, what
might get in the way?

How much do you really want it? Get in touch with your body, do a scan,
what are you feeling and where, pinpoint the joy as a physical feeling.

111

What's in it for you? How will your life change if you succeed in creating your perfect garden? What will you have then that you don't have now? What won't you have then that you do have now?

What are you risking? If you go for it and take the risks, what's the worst that could happen? If it did happen, what's the worst that could happen again, and again, and again, and again. Take this exercise to its final conclusion, the very worst that could happen – where are you? Still here and still surviving? Then the very worst scenario isn't going to kill you, so what's stopping you?

What does success look like to you?

Success is a very emotive word and can conjure up all sorts of visions and feelings for people. A lot of importance has been placed on being 'successful', but what does that mean exactly? Success is very personal and means different things to different people, we should never judge someone else's view of success for them.

Years ago I was working with an organisation that helped people who had been on the street get back into work and into 'normal' mainstream living that we all take for granted. One women who was supported during this process had been on the streets for over twenty years, she had lost contact with her children and had very low self-esteem as you would imagine. She had a two-week contract to work in a large supermarket chain, stacking shelves. Although there was never any expectation on the company to employ her after the two week work placement, her commitment, energy and clear enthusiasm for the job were so infectious that she was offered a full-time post. When asked what success meant for her, she said 'When I'm trusted enough to be on the till and handle money'. She was on the tills within six months. Her view of her own success was, rightly, huge. She had accomplished what had appeared totally out of her reach just twelve months previously when she had still been living on the streets.

Our personal journeys are a direct result of our view of the world and that is dependant upon our life experiences to date. We are all different, we have different challenges, different obstacles. Don't judge yourself against others, what is right for you and your view of success is perfect.

As I mentioned in Chapter One, I was married and divorced twice in my twenties. I could say I have two failed marriages behind me, or I could (and do) say I was successful in extricating myself from two relationships that were not supportive of me and were detrimental to my health and wellbeing.

Not only do I not view those experiences as failures, I also don't beat myself up about making the decision to marry both men. I recognise where I was in my life-journey at that point and why I made the decisions I did. I'm a different person today and would not make similar choices.

Before I ask you to think about what success means to you, I want to talk about money. A lot of people put a lot of store on material possessions and financial abundance around the area of success, other people believe that's not what success is about and think that it is wrong to want financial wealth. They are both opinions, neither right or wrong. But I do want to gently challenge anyone who may believe the accumulation of great wealth isn't right.

Money is not good or bad, it just 'is'. It is simply an energy that flows around the world. Because many people have a belief around lack, they think that they need to hang onto every penny otherwise they will lose it. They believe there's not enough to go round and then where will they be? You know what – there is plenty to go round. You actually don't own any of the money that's currently in your purse or Bank Accounts, you simply have temporary custody of it. It was with someone else before it was with you and will be with someone else after it's left you.

Imagine money as a stream of water. If you hold onto it and stop the flow of energy then the water becomes stagnant, starts to smell and kills off everything that lives in it. It you let the money go, knowing in your heart that there is plenty that will come your way to replace it, you keep the energy moving and the water flowing. The water remains clear, healthy and vibrant and everything in it grows and flourishes.

The desire to accumulate money however, does not make someone a bad person. As I said earlier, money is neither good or bad, it simply 'is'. It's what a person decides to do with it that matters. Money gives you choices that you wouldn't have otherwise. It gives you options to do more things, different things, to give back in a way that is right for you. So never understate its importance or feel guilty about wanting it. Try not to judge those who do have an abundance of money, as this is telling you how you view yourself far more than how you view them.

Do you believe you deserve wealth? If not, why not? You deserve whatever you desire.

I'd like you to start thinking about your own picture of success. Imagine that in later years you are looking back over your life. Describe what you will have done that will mean you consider your life has been successful.

I will consider my life has been successful if:

....

....

....

....

....

. . . .

. . . .

. . . .

. . . .

Energy Boosters and Energy Depleters

What are the things, people, experiences that boost your energy or deplete you of energy? Some examples from some of the programmes I've run are:

Energy Boosters

Children
Chocolate
Alcohol
Sex
My partner
Sunshine
Food
Dancing
Exercise
Laughter
Positive people
Being recognised for doing a good job
Sleep
Taking myself out of my comfort zone

Energy Depleters

Children
My partner
Alcohol

Food
Lack of exercise
Exercise
Bad weather
Negative people
Complainers
Conflict
Not being recognised for what I do
Fear
Lack of sleep
Not enough time
Bad drivers
Traffic jams
Late trains
Deadlines that are unrealistic
LIFE!

Usually Energy Depleters is the list that flows far more easily. But actually, nothing on either list will give or drain you of your energy. What a lot of people do on a regular basis is give their energy away to situations, people, events, things, over which they have absolutely no control. You are, in fact, far more in control over how your day goes than you think you are. What drains you of your energy is not the situation itself but rather your reaction to it. It is your reaction that you can control. And I don't mean that you are meant to be on an even keel all day every day, that's unrealistic. We all react to situations, that's part of being alive and it also keeps us safe. It's about making sure those reactions stay in context and do not become all consuming to the point that it has a detrimental effect on you. There will always be negative people in the world, that will never change sadly, but you can choose how much, if at all, they are going to impact on you and your life.

Weather, like money which I talked about earlier, is neither good or bad, it simply 'is'. If you live in a country where it rains a lot, then rain is deemed to be bad weather (unless you're a gardener or a duck!). But if you live in a country that sees very little rain then sun can be seen as bad weather and rain as wonderful. Weather itself is completely innocent.

I do quite a lot of driving, particularly motorway driving, and I see a lot of very 'interesting' driving skills. I used to let 'bad' driving really get to me, if someone cut me up or drove far too fast or did something stupid, I could feel my stress levels go through the roof. There is something about being in a car that changes people, you say things out loud you wouldn't dream of anywhere else! Of course, what happened then was that as I allowed my stress levels to rocket and stay high, I turned into the person I was cross at – a bad driver. The person who had 'made me stressed' had absolutely no idea that they had just ruined my day. Because, of course, I stayed in that elevated stress state and everything then went wrong for the rest of that day. I blamed it entirely on some stranger in a car who overtook me on the M25 at 9am that morning. How sensible was that?

I used to spend a lot of time 'blaming' other people for my stress levels, rather than taking responsibility for my reactions. By recognising that I am in control of my energy and emotions, and I don't have to give any of it away if I choose not to, is a much better way for me to live.

This doesn't mean that I don't see any bad driving, that I no longer react at all, and just smile and wave to everyone who cuts me up – I am human (with a very short temper!). But what happens now is that I allow myself to react, then bring my stress levels back down to normal very quickly. What doesn't happen any more is that I allow my stress levels to remain high longer than is appropriate. In other words, I let go of what isn't important and get my life into perspective. Inevitably some things happen in our lives that create long-term stress and we may need to get support during those times, but general day-to-day activity we really can control.

Now is the time for you to take back control of your life and make sure you don't give your energy away inappropriately to any of the wrong people.

I'm certain you are really healthy, fit and balanced. However, I want to share with you a piece of information that was told to me a few years ago. It really surprised me and my previous beliefs around bad cholesterol.

> Stress plays a much higher role than food on our
> bad cholesterol levels.

Stress releases adrenaline which creates cortisol which is a toxin. This is a toxin we can become addicted to, hence the adrenaline junkies out there. The trouble with cortisol is that it can create higher levels of bad cholesterol in the body.

Also, for some women, cortisol can actually create an 'armour' of fat around our middles to protect us. Some woman actually lose weight quite rapidly if they are stressed as they just burn if off. But if you fall into the other category, as I know I do, and you would like to avoid putting on weight, try and de-stress! Any diet and/or gym routine will automatically be far more effective if you can tackle your stress levels at the same time.

Are you addicted to stress? If your life is running too smoothly, do you create critical life events to add a bit of spice and interest? This can sometimes happen without people being consciously aware that they're doing it. Be really honest with yourself, is this a trap you sometimes, or often, fall into?

Think about what gives or depletes you of your energy.

Are they entirely appropriate?
What control could you take back for yourself?
Where can you achieve greater balance?
Are you addicted to stress?
What changes can you make to your reactions and actions?

Fear of success or fear of failure?

What do I mean by this? Well, a lot of people when asked to set themselves goals will have one of these lurking at the back of their subconscious that may get in the way.

Most people believe the obvious one is 'fear of failure' which can either motivate people to achieve or paralyse them into inaction. Quite often this comes from someone's background. They have a desire to move out of a certain situation, because the fear of staying there would mean they were a failure in their eyes. This can act as a strong pull to shake things up and do it differently. Fear of failure can also stop people taking any action at all. This can come from an 'internal message' that they are not good enough, and are bound not to succeed, so therefore what's the point of even trying and setting themselves to fail, surely it's better to not even start.

The only failure is not trying. Giving something a go and the end result not looking exactly how you had planned is not failure. Your goal is your goal, you are allowed to change the outcome if you want to. And about this 'not being good enough' – according to whom exactly? This is rubbish (which you know anyway).

The other one, fear of success, is interesting and not obvious, but can be just as debilitating and paralysing. A lot of people are frightened of success and the impact it may have on them and on the people around them.

What will people think if I'm too 'successful'?
Will they still like me?
Will they think I'm too big for my boots?
Will I lose friends?
Will people try to trip me up and bring me back down to earth?
Will I be 'found out' that I'm actually a fraud?

Powerful messages. So many people are frightened of being visible, of putting their head above the parapet and being seen, of waiting for someone to 'find them out' and say "hah! I knew you were a fraud!"

Both fear of failure and fear of success have their roots in the same emotion – lack of self belief.

Which one, if either, is within you?

Where did it come from?

Do you want to keep it?

If not, what do you need to do to delete it?

What do you want to have as your truth?

Are You Towards Motivated or Away From Focussed?

Whenever you set a goal for yourself, think about this. Let me give you an example. If someone has a goal to lose weight it's really helpful if they can pinpoint and be clear about their motivation.

If someone wants to lose weight because they have a fear of being overweight, of the comments they may get, the clothes they can't fit into and the fact that they believe they may be unattractive to existing or potential partners – then they are **away from focussed.**

Their key motivator is moving away from the fear of staying where they are.

If, on the other hand, they want to lose weight because they can see the joy of being slimmer, they feel the health and wellness they will have, they imagine the extra energy and joie de vivre they live with – then they are **towards motivated.**

Their key motivator is moving towards the joy of the end result.

Which one do you think is the most powerful? Well, they are pretty equal as motivators, but one will have much more power when you come up against any obstacles.

Why do you think most diets don't work? Because the majority of people (women) who go on them, are away from focussed. Their key motivator is moving away from the fear of being overweight, powerful to start the diet, but not very supportive when the first hurdle presents itself, because the long term motivator isn't there. They haven't fast forwarded themselves into their future when they've lost the weight, they haven't visualised themselves and the joy they will feel and the energy they will experience.

Had they done that at the beginning, then the hurdles would have been easier to overcome as they would have started the diet being towards motivated.

There is something I use with clients that proves to be very helpful, this is called Action Planning with the Change Equation, which illustrates what I've just talked about. This can be used in any area of your life, personal or business.

ACTION PLANNING
WITH THE
CHANGE EQUATION

The Change Equation is a simple formula which is often used to illustrate some of the important issues in bringing about successful organisational change. However, it can also be used to help people think through issues of individual change and development.

The Change Equation suggests that, by and large, people will resist or avoid change, because change often brings with it some level of pain or discomfort. In order to help people change, therefore, other and more positive factors need to be brought into the process.

It suggests that for productive change to occur

The sum of A + B + C must exceed the value of D, where:

A = An attractive vision of the future
B = Some dissatisfaction with the present
C = Some practical first steps
and
D = The pain involved in changing

On the following pages are some questions designed to help you think through some of the issues involved in your personal change and development.

Try to answer these questions for yourself, making notes as you go along. Some people prefer to do this alone; some welcome the chance to discuss the issues that arise.

As you do your thinking and make your notes, try to notice any of the major themes that come through, around which you can design an action plan.

Vision

Have I got a clear and attractive vision of how the future might be for me?

....

....

....

....

....

How can I best use my gifts?

....

....

....

....

Have I got a clear picture of what I want in life?

....

....

....

....

How can I clarify my vision – what help do I need to do that?

....

....

....

Dissatisfaction With The Present

How much do I enjoy my present role/situation?

....

....

....

What would I most like to change?

....

....

....

What is the basis of that dissatisfaction?

....

....

....

If I did change my role/the situation, what would I be leaving behind? How important is that to me?

....

....

....

Which has the greatest pull – the way things are at the present or the way they could be if I changed things?

....

....

How much do I really want change?

....

....

Some Practical First Steps

What things can I do SOON to move things forward?

Examples:

Gaining knowledge

Developing skills

Gaining different experience

Developing networks

Negotiating a different role/situation

Your Own Examples:

....

....

....

....

....

The Pain Of Changing

What is the magnitude of the change required?

....

....

....

What would be involved – for me and for others involved in the change?

....

....

....

What support do I, and others, need during this transition?

....

....

....

Support Network

Complete the following, naming which person in your work or personal life who fulfils that need:

Someone I can rely on in a crisis

....

Someone who makes me feel good about myself

....

Someone with whom I can be totally myself

....

Someone who will tell me how well or how badly I am doing

....

Someone I talk to if worried

....

Someone who really makes me stop and think about what I am doing

....

Someone who is lively to be with

....

Someone who introduces me to new ideas, new interests, new people

....

Your key driver

Which one is driving you:

Away from focussed ☐   Towards Motivated ☐

To finish up this chapter and, indeed, this part of the book which has been all about you and your own self-development and journey, I'd like you to start to visualise and create the future you want for yourself. Start to get really excited, again tune into your body and listen to what it's telling you.

Make a list of activities that you currently enjoy doing the most. These can be personal or business; they could include hobbies and activities that you find fulfilling or even things that you get really enthusiastic about.

What makes your heart sing? When do you get tingles in your body?

Some of the things that make my soul light up are:

Watching the sunset from my flat, I overlook the sea and the South Downs and the sunsets are magnificent, whatever time of year

Going for a walk beside the sea, really helps me to put my life into perspective

Spending time with girlfriends and laughing so much my face hurts and I think I'm going to be physically sick!

Receiving emails/cards/messages from clients letting me know what they've achieved, what's changed for them, their successes

Bumping into clients when they're not expecting to see me and seeing the joy radiating out of them

Watching *Strictly Come Dancing*

Taking myself out of my comfort-zone and realising my imagination was playing tricks on me

Now it's your turn.

My soul lights up when I

....

....

....

....

....

....

....

....

....

....

....

....

....

....

Well done! Having gone through this process myself, I know it isn't always easy to dig as deep as I've asked you to. But I also know how liberating it was to finally get rid of the demons and feel free to step into my light and shine in the world. I hope you're feeling lighter, re-invigorated and fresh. Onto Part Four now, how you can make a difference in the world of work – whatever that looks like for you.

Part Four
Using This In
The Real World

Chapter Nine
How We Think

'Here is a magical secret we all need to know:
People change. No-one is stuck who chooses not to be.
No-one is without infinite potential for a radical turnaround
from all that is unconscious and fearful and weak to all that is
conscious and loving and strong.'
Marianne Williamson

This chapter is about getting to grips with what makes you tick. Everyone has a natural, default communication style which regulates their view of the world and everyone in it. This impacts on how we deal with learning new tasks, our team-player ability, our individual leadership styles, what we find stressful or stress free, how we receive and give messages, how we filter the information we hear and decide what to pass on to other people.

It is not about operating from just one quarter of your brain, we are, obviously, our whole brain. It is simply that one quarter is likely to be your most preferred style of operating, with the other three quarters making up the backing group. This is truly individual for each of us and really fascinating once you start to dig deeper and discover what makes you and everyone else 'tick'.

The brain is divided into left and right, top and bottom. So the four potential quarters of the brain are as follows:

Top left

Top right

Bottom left

Bottom right

Each quarter will have a dominating personality style which is then complemented by the other three.

To be a good manager of people or business owner, it is imperative that you not only know where you are on this scale, but also where your team or clients are. Let's look at the characteristics of each quarter in more detail.

Top left

People with this as their dominant quarter are likely to be great visionaries and global thinkers. They are likely to be an expert in their chosen field, and like to work with other experts. They will probably 'test' other people and their knowledge. They love to know how things work, they are great at taking things apart and putting them back together again having figured out the mechanics and fine detail. Their favourite question is 'why'. In fact they question a lot, always searching for information and increased knowledge.

They prefer to work by themselves and are not the obvious social or networking personalities of a team or a group. They really hate being put on the spot to present information, so will always need notice if being asked to do so, they don't naturally like being the centre of attention, preferring to observe and do their own thing.

They can sometimes be viewed by other people as being rather stand-offish and unfriendly, they are not keen on sharing personal information and not obviously comfortable with 'feelings'. They may come across as being cold and unfeeling, they're not, they just have to build trust in people before they are willing to share anything.

They love research and detail, and are great at analysing from every angle and will definitely 'think before they speak'. They tend to process everything internally before it is shared with anyone.

Their greatest skills are expertise and clear, tunnel-visioned focus. They can always be relied upon to get things done and can be courageous leaders with an expansive vision.

Their greatest challenges are to be 'people' focused, to listen to the stories of others (and be interested!), to be spontaneous, take risks and be outwardly social.

Tips for working with them:

Cut the ….. and get to the point.

Talk in bullet points, not paragraphs, and particularly not novels

Do your research before presenting an idea. They will test your knowledge, and you will lose their respect if it's clear you don't know what you're talking about

If you make a mistake, be clear that you understand what went wrong and why, and what steps you are going to take to ensure it doesn't happen again

Give them their space and don't invade it unless invited to do so

Don't expect quick answers to your questions – they need time to process

Give them plenty of notice about anything and don't talk to them walking down a corridor on the way to a meeting.

Bottom left

People with this as their most preferred style will be hugely organised in every area of their life. They know exactly where everything is, how much is in their bank account at any given moment, they are the 'belt and braces' people of the world. Nothing is left to chance and preparation is key.

Similar to the top left style, these people will not naturally seek the limelight, preferring to stay in the background and get things done. They may well be seen as the foundations of a company or team, creating the solid base on which others can operate. They may be seen by others as being nit-picking and a bit bossy, but without them a group would collapse, we all need a solid foundation in order to flourish and blossom. These are not the risk-takers of the world, in fact they love rules and regulations and may be tempted to invent a few more if they believe there are not enough.

These people are lovers tradition, both personal and professional. They enjoy history and family is hugely important to them. When at work their team is their family and they care about every member greatly. Good, solid professions will make them happy, they are not natural entrepreneurs as the risk of not having a guaranteed salary may well be too much to contend with.

Their greatest skills are their dependability, loyalty, perfectionism, attention to detail, reliability and steadfastness.

Their greatest challenges are to be spontaneous, to go with the flow, take a few risks, relinquish control – of themselves and other people – and permit mistakes, again, of themselves and other people.

Tips for working with them:

Avoid too much frivolity at work and pointless conversations when in their company

Always make sure you are fully prepared if you have a meeting with them

Work to very clear deadlines – when giving them tasks and when completing tasks for them

Never run a meeting without an agenda – and make sure you stick to it

Always do what you say you are going to do and by the date you said you would do it

Try not to be too chaotic with your style of speech, work plans or instructions

135

Top right

People with this as their dominant quarter are, similar to top left people, great visionaries and global thinkers, they just come at it from a completely different standpoint. These people are the risk-takers, they push the boundaries, for themselves, and for the companies they run or work for. They are wonderful trouble-shooters, loving a challenge they can get stuck into, finding a new and unique way to overcome the issue. They are definitely 'glass half full' people, rarely letting doubt enter their vocabulary or thought processes, they believe there is always a way.

They are very social, and can be quite loud if they are extroverts. You definitely know they are around! They work much better with other people around them and they like noise and an element of chaos and unpredictability about their lives and surroundings.

They tend to talk more quickly than other people and can sometimes open their mouths before they have fully engaged their brains. This can lead them to land in hot water on regular and frequent occasions. But, as they possess great charm and self effacement, they usually get themselves out of sticky situations with humour and speed.

They are great fun to be around and will lift the energy of any group. Because of their optimism they will pull people out of the doldrums very quickly. However, if they are extreme in this quarter they can also be exhausting, they push themselves and expect everyone else to share their vision, energy and motivation. They don't take kindly to people trying to be 'sensible' and throwing a bucket of cold water over their ideas.

Their greatest skills are their flexibility, mobility, energy, and their ability to see things in a unique and revolutionary way. They test boundaries and strive for improvement. They are adaptable and able to change direction at a drop of a hat, therefore they cope very well, even thriving, with change.

Their greatest challenges are to slow down! To listen to other people and not assume they know everything. To both honour stability and respect rules. To practice patience and to understand the need for detail, and not try to fast-forward everything in their life to the end result.

Tips for working with them:

Get excited about their ideas even if you don't agree with them

Allow them to express their creativity

Give them short deadlines, they work much better under pressure

If there's a problem, give it to them, they love to trouble shoot and they come into their own when doing so

Allow them a voice – these are the best people to give presentations, talk in public, do the networking and build the contacts

Don't try and keep them quiet, they will become very disruptive, but don't let them take over either, they need firm handling

Bottom right

Those with this as their dominant quarter are the 'people' people of the world. They love being around people, are very intuitive and can walk into a room and immediately know who isn't feeling happy. They are natural communicators and nurturers, caring hugely how everyone else is feeling. They are more likely than anyone else to put other people first and themselves second. They love harmony and are not naturally good with conflict. They may get hurt easily and have a tendency to sulk. They may be perceived by others as being weak – not strong enough to lead. However, people under-estimate this group at their peril, these are very strong people, they simply show their strength in other ways. They are far more likely to adopt the coaching and empowering style of leadership than the command and control style. People are drawn to them because of their ability to communicate openly and their desire to pull a team together collaboratively.

They will hate working by themselves, much preferring the group set-up and team-building ethos. Because of the empowering and caring side to their leadership and management of others, they will always have a much better exit strategy than most in business. They have spent the time building the people underneath them to be able to take over when it's time for them to move onwards and upwards.

These are the leaders who will create a strong bond and firmly established loyalty within others. If you have this person leading a company, when times get tough everyone is far more likely to pull together and work to get through the rough patch because they won't want to let their leader down. A company led by these people will operate like a 'family' far more than a hierarchical, dominant and distant establishment.

Their greatest skills are their ability to pull people together, to create calm and harmonious environments. They naturally take people with them due to their people-skills and genuine interest in others.

Their greatest challenges are not to talk about their private lives too much. To understand boundaries, and not abuse them. To keep their language succinct and to the point, avoiding rambling conversations. To resist the urge to 'rescue' people.

Tips for working with them:

The three most important words for these people are 'please' and 'thank you', you forget these at your peril, they will never forget and rarely forgive

Validation is hugely important for this group, they really do need to know that they are doing a good job, take the time to tell them

Be sympathetic that they wear their hearts on their sleeve and don't slap them down verbally, and never in the presence of others, if you make them look stupid in public they will never speak to you again!

If you are led by someone like this, don't underestimate them and try and be 'clever'. They are powerful leaders, respect their personality and learn from it. These people represent the leaders of the future – caring, empowering, holistic, nurturing, communicators and inspiring. Actually, as women, what we naturally do exceptionally well.

If you are still doubting the importance of a particular quarter in the overall scheme of things, let me explain visually.

If you look at the tree above and divide it into four distinct parts:

The roots
The trunk
The branches
The leaves/fruit/flowers

What quarter of the brain would you associate with each part of the tree?

The roots = bottom left
The trunk = top left
The branches = top right
The leaves etc = bottom right

Why?

Because the roots of a tree represent the solid, firm foundation and roots of a company, team, group, unit of people. Everything bottom left people do brilliantly. Without firm roots, nothing will grow.

The trunk represents the vision of the tree, it's growing upwards and out into the world, but with solid conviction, taking its time and not rushing, doing what it needs to do to establish its strength and place in the world. Everything top left people do, and without a trunk nothing else will exist.

The branches are a bit random, crossing over each other, getting in each others way, making a statement, having their say. But they have far more flexibility than the trunk in that they can sway and change direction more easily, yet are still reaching for the stars with their vision. Just like the top right people.

The leaves, flowers, fruit etc. is the nurturing part of the tree, the part that feeds every creature that comes to it, including us if it's fruit. It creates the beauty, colour and gentle harmony of the tree and makes it 'whole'. Describing bottom right people perfectly.

Now let me ask you, what would happen to that tree if one part of it died or wasn't there? Answer – the whole tree would suffer and eventually it would all die. Every part of that tree is as important and crucial to the survival and strength of the whole as every other part. By working together and in harmony a tree produces a sustainable and repeatedly replicable version of itself and it takes a hurricane of magnitude to topple it.

Companies, teams, groups and individuals are the same. Diversity of character is crucial to the strength and survival of any group of people of whatever size. No-one is right or wrong, they simply 'are'. We are all a mixture of all four quarters, just in an entirely different percentage. If we disrespect someone else's character, we are actually disrespecting ourselves on some level. If we honour and celebrate someone else's character, then we are also honouring and celebrating ourselves.

How the above is applied within the business environment

This knowledge of the brain is translated in business terms as Personality Profiling. There are many different tools out there, and you've probably been through the process of at least one in your time. Even though they have different names and use a variety of words to describe the four quarters, they are essentially coming up with the same result.

Companies use these tools for a number of reasons:

For recruitment and to establish a person's suitability to a role and a particular environment

Team building – everyone appreciating everyone else

Communication skills

Customer service – understanding your customers, how they complain, and how they want to be treated is vital for any company of whatever size

Front-line/service-staff (for the above reasons)

Dealing with conflict in a team or business relationship, ie how to deal with your boss and how to deal with your team

Personal career development – being aware of your natural strengths and where your potential challenges may lie

It is particularly useful for people running their own companies when you have to be everything to everyone at the beginning

The impact for you in the workplace

A good manager of people or entrepreneur will have a clear knowledge of their natural strengths and areas of potential challenge. This demonstrates pro-active business skill, someone who takes ownership and responsibility for their own growth and learning.

If you are not aware of who you are, you run the risk of the following:

Not being aware of your limitations

Not knowing what, and to whom, to delegate

Not knowing who you need to grow underneath you

Not knowing what may stop you in your tracks and allow you to lose confidence in your abilities

Remember no-one is right or wrong, they just 'are', it is crucial that all managers of people and businesses take the responsibility to know this information.

If you do not take the time to know your team and your colleagues, or your clients, how are you going to grow them and empower them to be the best they can be? How are you going to delegate the right task to the right person and light them up, rather than close them down? Do you carry out all appraisals, development plans and one-to-one meetings in exactly the same way with everyone? Do they all go as successfully as each other? If not, have you ever wondered why? People are not the same and cannot be treated or managed as such. The power is in diversity and individuality – recognise that, and celebrate that, and you will become charismatic and a magnet for excellence.

If you have never gone through any personality profiling, I strongly suggest you do so as quickly as possible. They are enlightening and truly helpful, not just in the work-place but in every area of your life.

You may well have recognised yourself in the descriptions I gave of the four quarters, but remember – you are all of them, it's just that one is likely to be dominant, your most preferred style. I am equal in top and bottom right, about sixty five percent of my brain preference is the right side and I know I struggle with research, data, broad time-scales, and budgets. So as soon as I could afford to, I outsourced those aspects of my business. But I also know that if I honour every part of 'me' my life runs more smoothly.

If I am going to see a potential new client, I will become very top left, I do my research of the company and the person I am going to see.

When getting ready for the appointment or for a training course, I become very bottom left, I plan and right lists and tick everything off as I pack it. I check time scales, agendas, how I'm going to get there, how long it will take me etc.

When I arrive and run the training programme this then allows me to step into my most preferred right brain activities.

Being self-employed honours my top right desire for spontaneity, taking risks and being in control of my destiny. Doing what I do, working with people and empowering them to be the best they can be, honours my bottom right desires.

Accessing Your Least Favourite Style At Work

On the following pages are some activities you could undertake to strengthen your least favourite styles. These will help you achieve a greater balance.

Top Left Activities

When making a decision, use analysis

Spend time with the 'techies' in the company, learn their language and how they operate

Read and understand the annual report

Calculate your salary by the minute

Become proficient at a new computer programme that would enhance your skills

Have clearly defined business goals for the next financial quarter

Top Right Activities

Come up with at least one 'crazy' idea every day

Close your eyes and imagine your company ten years from now

Add visual creativity to your work space

Design a logo for your job

Make a decision based purely on intuition and 'gut'

Invent a new product for the company

Use pictures and colour to plan a meeting

Bottom Left Activities

Use a time-log and precisely record your activities in a day

Organise and tidy your filing system and/or your work space

Create a 'things to do' list and tick off when completed

Set a time for completing a project, then finish it early

Arrive earlier than the designated appointment time

Read the Policies of the Company and refer to it when needed

Don't make rash decisions

Bottom Right Activities

Become aware of your non-verbal communication and ensure it is friendlier and more approachable

Take time to get to know other people you work with on a personal level

Come to a team decision using debate

Recognise people you work with and their achievement and make the recognition personal

Ask colleagues about their weekend, listen and be genuinely interested in their answer

Give praise whenever and wherever you can.

It can be a challenge to operate from your least-preferred style I know. But if you can manage to balance yourself and honour every aspect of who you are and how you operate in the world, it makes it so much easier to celebrate others. You are easier to be around, people will naturally want to work harder for you and ultimately you create success on a much broader scale.

What is really important for women in the world, is that we have a voice, a voice that reflects our confidence, authority and magnetism. In the next couple of chapters I will take you through the various ways in which you can express that voice and have your say.

Chapter Ten
A Voice With Confidence

'The fastest way to change society is to mobilise the women of the world.'
Charles Malik, former President of the United Nations General Assembly

This is not about simply speaking in public, although that is part of it. Having a voice with confidence really encompasses everything about being great in the world. It allows you to have your say, get noticed, to put your head above the parapet and not be afraid of being visible.

In this chapter I concentrate on : public speaking and internal meetings. In the next chapter I expand this to include networking and raising your profile.

All of the above are ways you can, and should, have a voice. It is crucial people know who you are, that you are the person they immediately think of for a particular skill, piece of advice, to lead, to get them out of a hole, for inspiration.

Public speaking

Let's start with what most people, male or female, think is the most scary. You may never have to do this, but it's a really good idea if you can find the opportunity to speak to an audience. As daunting as it may seem before the event, after you've done it the sense of achievement is huge. We all know our imagination plays tricks on us, what seems insurmountable at the start is achievable if we believe strongly enough in ourselves. If you've never spoken in public, please find the opportunity to do so quickly, if one doesn't naturally appear, create the opportunity.

I'm going to go through the different aspects of speaking in public:

When – Planning Your Talk – Preparing The Voice

When

What sort of opportunities present themselves to you? This may vary depending on whether you are employed or run your own business, but these are some of them:

External Conference

External Seminar

Internal Conference

Internal Seminar

Induction for New Employees

Induction for Graduates

External Networking (I'll cover this, and the next point, in more detail later in the next Chapter)

Internal Networking

Meetings

Client Entertaining

Guest Speaker at an Industry Event

After-dinner Speaker

Are there any other opportunities you can think of that are specific to where you work or the business you run? Capture them here

....

....

How many of the above are you able to volunteer to speak at? Don't assume that because you are not automatically asked to speak that you cannot volunteer. If you haven't raised your profile sufficiently, people may not instantly think of you when they need a speaker. It is up to you to be prepared to step forward and make yourself available and willing to participate. Once you've done this for the first time, you catapult yourself into people's consciousness as being the person to go to when someone of authority is needed.

People of influence are not made just because they have the knowledge. It is up to you to communicate your knowledge in the wider arena. The more you share your knowledge with others, thereby increasing your output, the more you will be respected for what you know.

How many people do you know, or have known, who have great knowledge and capability? But they keep themselves to themselves, they never put their heads above the parapet or dip their toe in the water of self-promotion. Because of their hesitancy to be visible, they are always overlooked and don't progress to the level that their knowledge and expertise justifies.

Don't let that person be you.

People don't know you're out there, are not aware of your knowledge, skill, talents and expertise unless you tell them.

We all know that promotion and success should go to the best person for the job based on skill and experience. We also all know that isn't always the case. The people who generally get the best jobs, the quickest promotions, the greatest deals, and the fastest business success are the people who get noticed. Their external output is consistent, focused and visible.

Don't wait to get noticed by the people who matter. They're too busy to seek you out, they want you delivered to them on a plate!

Where could you find the opportunity to have a voice, speak in public and share your knowledge?

....

....

....

What's stopping you going for it *now?*

....

....

....

What can you do, or who can help you, overcome these obstacles and *just do it?*

....

....

....

Planning your talk

Once you've created the opportunity for yourself and have it booked in your diary, you need to plan your talk.

How long are you expected to talk for?
To how many people?
What time of day, so flavour of the talk?
What are you talking about?
What style are they expecting?
What equipment do you need and who is supplying it?

149

How long?

This is crucial, it may be all they want is a quick ten minute summary to open an event, close a conference, introduce a subject etc, or they may require a full and in-depth lecture lasting an hour or more. The longer the time the easier it can be to plan. Getting your key points across in a short time-scale can be trickier to plan and needs careful thought.

Be aware of your key points though, so however long you are talking you ensure these are communicated to your audience. What are the main points you want them to take away from what you are saying? The audience needs to have these clearly in their minds whether you are talking for ten minutes or two hours.

To how many?

You may think that the smaller the audience the easier it is going to be. The reality is the opposite, actually the more people you are talking to the easier it is. I know this sounds ridiculous, surely an arena of hundreds is far more intimidating that a room of ten?

When you have a small audience, you will have eye-contact with everyone, which on one level is great, it creates an atmosphere of connectedness and familiarity and everyone has the opportunity to speak to you afterwards. The potential downside of this scenario is that if, for whatever reason, someone in the room doesn't like what you are saying (they've got out of the wrong side of the bed that day, had a row with a loved one etc) because you have eye-contact with everyone, you will be aware of it.

This may put you off your stride, speaking to a small audience is a lot more personal, for them and for you. But don't let that put you off speaking to small groups, it doesn't often happen and if you know your subject (which of course you do) it won't topple you off balance. But it's good to be aware of the possibility, so that if it does happen you can deal with it internally and carry on like a professional.

Speaking to a large audience IS easier. I know that when I was told this at the beginning of my public-speaking career I thought the person who told me was mad. The thought terrified me and I wanted to keep to the small, intimate groups where I felt safe.

Then I was asked to talk on Personal Branding and Style in a theatre to about 600 people. Of course I said 'Yes', even though I felt sick every day for weeks beforehand and thought my legs would give way as I was waiting to go on stage. I'd only been speaking to audiences for about six months, this was baptism by fire! But on I went, with a microphone, standing in the middle of the stage, all on my own, with the spotlights on me and looking out at a sea of black.

I could only make out people in the front couple of rows, everyone else was invisible, so it was like talking to a small group anyway. I spoke for an hour in the lovely bubble of self-belief that everyone in the theatre loved what I was saying. Because, frankly, as I couldn't see them anyway, I had absolutely no idea if they liked me or not. If someone didn't like what I was saying, I couldn't see them or hear them and therefore was not aware of them. Bliss! But I heard laughter in the right places and everyone (I think) clapped at the end, so as far as I was concerned I'd been a huge success.

Whatever the size of your audience, don't let it put you off, you CAN speak in a theatre to thousands, trust me, I know you can do it because I have, and if I can do it – SO CAN YOU! I wasn't born being a public speaker, it's something I've had to learn over the years, I also had no formal training in public speaking so I really learnt the hard way, by making mistakes, by realising what didn't work and making sure I didn't do it that way again. I also watched other people speaking in public, I made a note of what they did that really worked, and adapted those skills for myself, and also what really didn't work, and made sure I didn't follow their example.

What time of day?

This may seem a strange thing to have to consider, but it does make a difference. If you are speaking at a breakfast meeting or event for example, everyone there is very focused and time-aware. These events are usually very early (obviously, it's over breakfast) and before the normal work start time. The audience want a talk that is succinct and to the point and doesn't overrun, they need to get out on time and get to the office. These talks are likely to be shorter, usually ten to twenty minutes maximum, so getting your key points across is essential here.

A lunchtime talk is similar but a little more relaxed, there may be alcohol involved, but probably not much as everyone has to return to the office. They are still time-focused though, so be clear on your message. You are likely to have longer to speak, anything up to thirty to forty minutes.

An evening talk is probably the most relaxed, people will have eaten beforehand so you don't have the hunger of your audience getting in the way of them listening to what you have to say! This is likely to be the longest time opportunity – anything up to an hour, and offers the greatest opportunity for you to talk to people afterwards as there is inevitably a period of networking that will follow your talk.

An after-dinner talk is possibly the most challenging. Everyone there will probably have been drinking, and more than they would do at lunchtime. They are very relaxed and want to be entertained, but you will have to work harder at entertaining them than at any other time of the day. This is when using humour in your talk will have the greatest impact, and any audience participation that you can include will keep them involved and awake. But if you notice any droopy eyes don't take it personally, it will likely be down to one too many glasses of wine!

Of course there are other time opportunities, during morning and afternoon sessions when you may be part of a programme of speakers or simply there to emphasise part of the day, or opening an event.

Make sure your talk can be adapted to each of the above time scenarios whilst keeping your key message clear and strong.

What are you talking about?

Are you being asked to be the expert, or are you giving your perspective on a subject the audience has a similar awareness of as yourself? It's good to know the level of expectation of your audience, what do they want to get out of listening to you? If you meet their expectations you will produce a brilliant talk.

It could be that the audience know very little, or nothing at all, about your subject. They will look to you as the expert in your field and look forward to learning from you, and how they can apply that information in their own lives.

It may be that everyone has a similar knowledge and understanding as yourself. You are there to give your viewpoint, to update them on the latest findings, to educate them on the latest forecasts, to set the scene for next steps and actions.

The scenario might be that you are there to entertain, you need to find the humour and fun factor of your subject and leave your audience with the feel good factor.

You could be talking to people higher up the organisation/industry/sector to you and you're presenting new ideas, better ways of working, the latest research etc.

Be aware of what your audience are expecting from you, how much knowledge and information they may or may not have about your subject, and how detailed you need to make your talk. If you're speaking to people in your industry, you can be far more detailed and industry specific, try and avoid using jargon at all costs, but there will inevitably be some words and phrases that you will all understand.

Be careful not to fall into the trap of assuming that your audience knows your subject. What can come across badly are speakers who talk in jargon and industry 'speak', whilst assuming that everyone listening understands them fully. Invariably this will divorce you from your audience and alienate you from building any rapport or relationship with anyone afterwards. It is also very aggressive be-haviour as it creates an environment of fear and lack of self-belief in everyone else, they are frightened to ask a question as this will show up their lack of knowledge and therefore they end up feeling stupid and put the blame entirely on the speaker – and rightly so.

Something to also be aware of is that if you are successful in getting your key points across, people will remember – for a long time.

I have been giving talks to audiences since 1989, and it's been won-derful to me that I have met people sometime after a particular talk who have quoted back to me – verbatim – parts of my speech. Sometimes the talk they attended was over ten years previously. They have told me the impact a certain phrase or sentence had on them. That something I said changed the way they thought about themselves or motivated them to take a particular course of action. As a result of some talks people have also tracked me down some considerable years later as they needed someone with my skill set, and the first person they thought of was me.

Never underestimate the power of your words.

What style are they expecting?

Is it an informal meeting with everyone sitting down and handouts given to everyone?

Is it very formal with a PowerPoint presentation? (Which should only be used to highlight each topic by the way, not be a visible version of what you're saying.)

Is it relaxed but structured, they're sitting and you're standing?

Is it very much a Keynote Speaker environment where you carry a lot of authority?

Find out before you arrive as this will help when planning your con-tent and also with what you wear, different styles will require a dif-ferent visual 'uniform'. Remember, it is the expectations of your audience that are always at the forefront of your planning.

Will you need any equipment?

The potential black hole of disaster for any speaker. If you do need to use equipment, try and take your own, you've used it before and you know how it behaves. Make sure you arrive in plenty of time to set up and test it, getting the projector in the right position for example.

If you're using someone else's equipment, get there even earlier, as there are far more chances of something going wrong. And always have a back up plan. Make sure you can deliver your talk without the use of equipment if you have to. Remember the point above – PowerPoint is ONLY there to introduce each topic of your talk and give the audience the occasional visual image to emphasise a point. So you should never be relying on it to give the presentation for you.

Preparing The Voice

So, you're confident with all of the above, you know what you're talking about, to whom, the time of day, for how long, and what your audience is expecting. The equipment's sorted, you look fabulous, you have business cards and brochures with you, your smile is in place, and you're ready.

Then the legs go weak, the throat dries up, the hands get sweaty, the heart starts beating at least twice as quickly, the stomach does somersaults, you open your mouth and out comes a tiny squeak.

Yikes!

What you need to do *first* is

Prepare a Voice that Captivates.

Breathing: The first step towards a powerful and captivating voice.

You can speak only as well as you breathe.

Control your breath and you begin to control your speaking voice. Also, better breathing reduces tension in the neck and shoulders that can inhibit your best natural voice. The voice is a wind instrument, try the following exercises to get yours in tune.

Get ready.

Stand with your feet not quite shoulder-width apart, relax and shake out any tension in arms and legs. Move your weight forward, more on the balls of the feet than the heels. Relax your hands by your sides. Start to pay attention to your breathing. As you exhale, release your shoulders, relax your neck, unclench your teeth, and see if you can manage a yawn and maybe even a smile.

Diaphragmatic breathing.

This is breathing from your belly. It fuels your voice and releases tension from your upper body. It's also called belly breathing because as you inhale, your belly expands (and your chest and shoulders don't move). This is alien to most women as we spend most of our lives sucking our stomachs in and not releasing them for all the tea in China! But if you want to watch pure diaphragmatic breathing, watch a baby, we are all born with the natural instinct to breathe this way, it's just that we 'unlearn' it as we go through life. If you do yoga or singing or meditation, you will be aware of this process and will probably already be doing it.

Place one hand over your belly button. Slowly inhale one long breath through your mouth while silently counting 'One... two... three... four...'. Your stomach should expand, pushing your hand forward (your shoulders and chest should not move). Feel your hand move out as you pull the breath deep into your lungs. Now, hold that breath and count silently, 'One... two... three... four...'. Next, exhale the breath through your mouth while counting silently 'One... two... three... four...'.

156

Do this until you are comfortable and breathing easily. Now, you're ready to start making a sound.

'Ha ....'

You are going to make a gentle 'Ha' sound, using up an entire breath on just that one sound. Take in a full belly breath, and as you exhale say a very gentle and quiet sustained 'Haaaaaa ...' until you run out of air. Do it again, being certain to really open your mouth as you softly sustain the 'Ha'.

Shoulder bounce.

Once you've mastered the 'Ha', start to release tension from your neck and shoulders. First, lift your shoulders up toward your ears, hold them for a count of four, and then let them drop, completely releasing them. Now, do this rapidly.

Next, combine the should bounce with the 'Ha'. With your hands relaxed by your sides, take a full belly breath and then exhale a gentle sustained 'Haaa', running out of air as you did before. Only this time, while you are doing the 'Ha', simultaneously do the shoulder bounce for the entire time you are making sound. This will help release tension from your vocal cords and help you prepare your voice to speak.

Keep it up.

Doing these exercises regularly will help prepare your breath to support your voice. Each time you do them you improve your breathing and release some of the tension that can easily accumulate through-out the day. They will help you prepare to speak, not just physically but also mentally, by reducing any anxiety you may be feeling.

Before you give your talk, try the pencil technique

This comes with a warning – don't do it in front of your audience. Go somewhere private - a cubicle in the ladies loo for example.

It is, however, an extremely effective technique for increasing your vocal clarity. Get a pencil or pen and hold it horizontally between your teeth and try and read the first paragraph of your talk as clearly as possible whilst stretching (really stretching) your cheek muscles as much as you can – the more painful the better, sorry! A couple of minutes of this will greatly increase your vocal clarity and articulation. Prepare to be amazed – it really does work.

Putting musicality and interest into your voice

I'm sure you've listened to some speeches where the speaker talks in a monotone, barely opening their mouth and putting no emphasise or variety in their voice at all. It's SO boring to listen to isn't it?

Remember, ninety three per cent of our message is received by how we say the words, with words themselves only representing about seven per cent. So it's not just what you are saying, but more importantly, how you are saying it. Your voice is an instrument and is capable of great variety, tone, speed, pitch, interest and musicality.

Ensure that your talk encapsulates the full spectrum of variety your voice is capable of producing. To keep your audience captivated and hanging on your every word, prepare your words as follows.

Look at your written speech and look for the key words – the words that convey the core of your message and underline them or type them in bold.

Now look for appropriate places to pause and also where you can use eye-contact to give extra emphasis (this can be very effective when used in conjunction with a pause). It is also useful to mark in breathing points in the pauses.

Example

'**Good afternoon** (PAUSE) I hope that you are enjoying this book (PAUSE and look around) my name is Katie and this afternoon I'd like you to put some of the things that you've learned so far (PAUSE) about planning your talk and voice (PAUSE) into practice in a short presentation. (PAUSE). **Many people** (PAUSE) when they get up to speak (PAUSE) are very nervous (PAUSE then Speed Up) but if you have practised the confidence-building techniques that I've written (PAUSE) then I'm sure (Slow) that you are not going to feel too nervous. (PAUSE).

I very much hope that you will find this exercise useful (PAUSE) and people will look forward very much to hearing what you have to say.'

This is very much an 'over the top' example to illustrate the effects of stress, pause, speed, eye-contact etc, but it is useful to emphasise the importance of being aware of these techniques and to understand the essential quality of rhythm when you are speaking to a group of people.

Anchoring your confidence

There is a technique you can do, that if done regularly, will really help you to put yourself into a positive, confident state before you go and face your public.

How do you do it?

All you have to do is remember a *specific* moment when you were supremely confident. It doesn't matter when or where you were but it is important to recreate that situation exactly in your mind. To *see*, *hear* and *feel* precisely what was happening in your mind at that moment when you were feeling this emotion of confidence.

Do be careful about the memory you conjure up though. A training colleague of mine was doing this exercise with a group of men and one chap volunteered himself to go through the exercise in front of the others. He got his memory very clearly identified and fixed in his mind, he followed the process and promptly started swaying and

159

speaking with a slurred voice. When asked what memory he had conjured up, he told everyone it was when he was 'Down the pub with my mates, having drunk about nine pints and I felt on top of the world.'

Think through the scenario carefully before taking yourself back there, particularly if you're in company!

Once you have got the sensation of confidence then close your eyes, if they are still open, and start to feel that feeling increase.

Now start to throw this sensation around your body, running from your head to your feet and back up again. Increase the feeling even more. You may want to start counting from one to ten, raising the feeling of confidence in your body with each number.

Now open your eyes and look round the room until the image has gone. Repeat this several times.

Finally, open your eyes and lose the image again and decide on a simple signal that you can use that could put you quickly back into this supremely confident state. It's called an 'anchor'. The anchor is a physical gesture – anything from squeezing your finger to giving your thigh a pinch.

When you feel that you have reached your maximum state of confidence 'fire your anchor' ie operate your signal. Again, repeat several times and then open your eyes, look around the room, and lose the feeling.

Next, picture where you would like to carry this confidence with you. This may be a meeting, a conference, a public speaking situation, a job interview or just everyday living.

Now fire your anchor and increase that feeling of confidence once more.

You will be over flowing with confidence that you can use whenever you need it.

Practice this process as much as you can in order that you are able to produce confidence whenever you need it.

Remember: with just one squeeze of your finger you can be ready to conquer the world!

Meetings

These can be internal or external, team meetings, meetings with clients etc. They may be led by you or by someone else. You may well be the only woman there.

When you are leading the meeting

In theory this is the easier scenario for you, you're in charge after all, so you call the shots. But there are areas of potential trickiness and some things that need to be taken into consideration:

Keeping to the agenda – how's your time-management? Be clear about the purpose of the meeting, who needs to do what, by when and who is going to make them accountable. How many meetings have you attended when nothing of note is said, no actions were taken and it was a waste of everyone's time? Don't let that happen if you're in charge.

Make sure you have authority with impact. Is your body-language supporting you?

Managing potential saboteurs, the people who try and trip you up. These are the people who would rather be leading the meeting themselves, or people who talk too much and take the meeting away from the agenda.

Let's take each one step-by-step.

What's you're time-management like? If you go back to the previous chapter on the brain, where do you see yourself? Are you naturally limbic left, therefore very organised, structured and time aware? Or are you more cerebral right, a bit scatty, can go off on tangents and love creative thinking that isn't bound by rules?

Be aware of who you are, what you are good at in terms of organising and running a meeting and where your potential challenges may lie. Then put in place strategies to cope with the challenges. If you rehearse the challenges before they appear you are much better placed to deal with them should they show up.

If you have problems with organisation, then ask someone for help. Delegate the task to a person who will shine and give them the opportunity to excel.

Perhaps you struggle to keep meetings on track because you enjoy exploring other areas of thought, and relish the conversations that go with them. If this is you, ask someone to give you a two minute warning before you need to move onto the next item on the agenda.

Be aware before you start the meeting what the ideal outcome is. Then never lose sight of that. Why are you all getting together, what is everyone going to get out of it and where do you go as a result? Knowing these before you start will help with the time-management and focus.

If there are action steps that arise from the meeting, ensure everyone is aware of what they are expected to do and by when. Clear guidelines for you and everyone else will take away areas of uncertainty. Then make sure you stick to your side of the bargain. If you get easily distracted, get someone to keep you accountable and check that you've done what you said you were going to do and by when.

Authority with impact. What is your body-language like? I'll cover this in more detail in the next chapter under networking, but if you are running the meeting your body-language must be giving everyone else in the room that information. If you're not sure how you come across to other people, ask someone you work with who you know and trust, to give you some feedback.

Do you come across as rather passive and introverted, and therefore give others a chance to take over and monopolise the meeting? If you recognise that you sometimes fall into this category, try the anchoring technique earlier in this chapter before the meeting starts. Be aware of who may try and take over and find strategies to minimise the chances of them doing that.

Do you come across as rather 'bossy' as you hate to relinquish control? If so, where does this come from, and what are you worried about?

That someone else will have something more important to say and you don't want to get 'found out'?

That you are the only person in the room who talks any sense anyway, so why let anyone else speak?

You are very organised and structured and hate anyone taking you away from your stream of thought.

You believe there is no room for spontaneity or creative thinking in the workplace.

Be conscious of the above thoughts, being bossy and always in control does not equal authority with impact, it equals people getting hacked-off and you losing their respect.

Authority with impact means:

That you are always present in the room. By this I mean you are not thinking about what you could be doing instead of being at the meeting. People will pick this up. Fill your space appropriately and with the right energy. Leave any negative thoughts outside of the door and enter with positive vibes.

You invite people into their space and allow them the freedom to express themselves without judgement.

Using charm, not control, to get results.

Having great eye-contact. Look at everyone attending when they enter, during the meeting and at the end.

Use active listening. Make sure you don't form your reply in your head while someone else is speaking, but really listen to them.

Be firm but fair – you allow expression of opinion by others, but you keep everyone focused.

Managing potential saboteurs

These are the people who sneer at others while they are speaking. But, remember they are telling everyone in the room exactly how they feel about themselves, *not* how they feel about you. The reality is that their personal self-esteem is so low they have to put other people down in order to feel good.

But I appreciate this can be very difficult to hang onto when you're in the situation.

So, what to do? Well, first off, don't get into a control-struggle with them, this will fire-up their energy and exacerbate their behaviour. Also, don't ignore them, the effect is likely to be the same. Try not mirror their behaviour by putting them down in front of others and trying to trip them up. All of this will result in you losing your authority and consequently the respect of everyone else there.

Remain cool, calm and assertive, own your space, own your knowledge and own your authority.

Know that they are feeling rubbish and try and find ways to help them feel better about themselves. They must be good at some aspect of their job otherwise they wouldn't be there, so make sure you can offer praise when appropriate. Be aware of their natural strengths – where are they in relation to their communication and dominant brain preference? Make sure you delegate appropriate tasks that will play to their natural strengths and make them feel important and wanted.

If you have children, how do you deal with them when they're having a tantrum? OK, I know you can't put people at work onto the naughty step, but you can implement some of the same techniques. What they need to learn is respect – for themselves first, then they can expand that out to others.

If you are aware of these people before the meeting, ask for support from someone else before you start. Get someone else to help take the heat off and divert attention away from both of you.

Try and change the energy. What do I mean by this? I don't know if you've ever watched *The Dog Whisperer* on the TV? A wonderful man in the US who helps people deal with their difficult pets. Now I'm not saying these saboteurs are dogs (hush my mouth) but actually it's amazing how the principles can be transferred to work with people.

This man is very in tune with dog behaviour and instantly picks up when they are about to misbehave/get aggressive etc. He simply changes the energy by doing something to distract them, it instantly changes their mood and they return to equilibrium.

So if someone is 'kicking off' and causing trouble, just change the energy. I don't mean talk louder than they are or getting into a dialogue, this can be done without saying a word. Do something that distracts them and takes the attention away from them. Can you stand up and retrieve something from your work bag/handbag/jacket? Or simply pour yourself a glass of water, anything that will draw the attention back to you. It's amazing how powerful this is, you haven't got into a confrontation with them, shouted them down, or created more tension. You've calmly and with gentle authority, changed the energy.

When someone else is running the meeting

In the previous situation you *have* to speak, but in this scenario you may not have to. This has the potential to present you with a difficult situation in which to have a voice. Here are some tips for making it easier:

Research, if it isn't obvious, who is going to be at the meeting. Make contact with them beforehand, this is especially beneficial if you haven't met any of the attendees before. If you know them already, arrange to arrive at the meeting with one of them. Then you are already speaking and it's easier to continue.

Say 'Hello' to everyone there before the meeting starts. Whether you know them or not, make physical and verbal contact, smile, shake hands, whatever. Ensure everyone in the room knows you exist. Even if you don't say anything else during the meeting, everyone will have been aware of your presence. Do the same at the end, say 'Goodbye', shake hands, make a comment about something they said etc.

Know what the meeting is about and what's on the agenda, then come up with a question or comment about one of the items, preferably early on. Email the meeting leader beforehand and ask that time is given to you to ask your question or make your point. You are guaranteeing yourself a voice even if you keep quiet for the rest of the meeting.

Try and talk immediately the meeting starts, even if it has nothing whatsoever to do with why you're all there. Simply asking someone to pass the water will do. This is not about content, it's about you opening your mouth and sound coming out – people need to be aware that you are in the room. Once you've started speaking it's much easier to talk again when you have something important to say.

Show that you are listening to other people. If they say something you agree with, tell them 'I really liked that point', 'Yes I agree' 'Absolutely'. It doesn't really matter what you say, it's all about saying something. Plus if you praise other people, they will automatically look to you when are they are speaking again, because we all want praise. This will instantly include you in the conversation and people will turn and wait for your response. You can have an active participation in the meeting without having to contribute a huge amount.

Ultimately it's all about making your mark quickly, the longer you leave it the harder it is to find your voice.

Experiment with the above, see what works for you, what doesn't, find your own ways and remember:

YOU HAVE A VOICE, A STRONG VOICE, A VOICE THAT DESERVES TO BE HEARD

Let's move on now to how you can use your strong voice to be more visible in the world.

Chapter Eleven
Being Visible

'The ladder of success is best climbed by stepping on the rungs of opportunity.'
Ayn Rand

This chapter extends the previous one. This is about having another kind of voice, having a presence both internally and externally, about making sure people know you are out there, establishing your authority and making your mark.

In this chapter I will be talking about Networking and Raising Your Profile.

Networking

A word that can instil fear and dread in many a strong woman. Most people hate doing it, will try and find ways to get out of it and think it's a waste of time.

Most people also have a completely wrong view of what it actually is. We are all used to, and aware of, the 'formal' networking situations: conferences, seminars, business groups, meet-and-greets, client events.

But networking is something you are doing all the time. It doesn't have to be formal and structured. In fact the best networking takes place when it isn't planned, formal or structured. It's the spontaneous, unexpected situation you find yourself in. It's all about being:

Alert – Awake – Aware

Alert to our surroundings and everything that is going on around us, let's face it women *do* have eyes in the back of their head, so this should be easy for us!

Awake to the possibility of all conversations, you never know where they might lead, who that person knows or the impact a few words from you can make.

Aware that all your conversations are networking conversations, be fully present whoever you are talking to (you also don't know who might be standing behind you and listening).

One of my examples

I was standing in the queue at the checkout of a well-known national store in their café, and the woman at the till complimented me on my clothes and the colours I was wearing. Rather than simply saying 'Thank you', I also told her it was part of what I did for a living. This immediately sparked interest and she asked me more, then she asked me if I could do anything about their uniforms as they all hated the colour. I said, 'Give me the name of the person in charge of making the decisions and I'll see what I can do.' She did. All from buying a cappuccino and a blueberry muffin!

Be open to the possibility that some of your best 'networking' conversations will happen while you're waiting for the lift, standing in the queue at the staff restaurant, waiting for your train/bus/tube, buying your daily paper. Open your eyes, your ears and invite the joy of expectation into your life – you never know who you might meet.

Of course, there are times when we all have to attend the formal, structured networking events, and having the tools to deal with these successfully can be hugely helpful.

Formal Networking – what it is and what it isn't

What it is:

Building rapport, establishing relationships, broadening your horizons, helping others, fun

What it isn't:

*Selling, marketing yourself, gossiping with friends,
only working to your agenda*

How many networking events have you attended in the past where someone comes up to you, without introduction or any prior contact, and thrusts their business card in your hand?

There is some seriously bad networking etiquette out there. A lot of people make the (wrong) assumption that networking is there to acquire as many business cards as they can and distribute as many of their own as they can. This is wrong on so many levels.

Networking is not a race to see how many 'contacts' you can accumulate in a given length of time. It's also not about who you might want to see again and who might call you – this isn't speed dating.

True networking is about:

Long-term contact

Expanding your knowledge of who is out there, what they do and how they can be of help and support to the other people you know

Building rapport

Establishing mutually beneficial relationships

Having a genuine interest in other people

Being visible in the business world for the right reasons

Ensuring you are the person others immediately think of as being 'well connected'

There is nothing more off-putting than someone talking about themselves all the time if they haven't been invited to do so.

There is nothing more alluring and magnetic than someone who is asking you to talk about yourself and is genuinely interested in what you say.

However, knowing all this doesn't necessarily make walking into a room full of strangers any easier.

But if you can take the spotlight off yourself for a second, and instead of thinking:

'I have nothing to say, I don't know anyone, no-one will want to talk to me.'

Try going in with the internal message:

'I wonder who I might meet and what interesting stories they might tell me?'

'I wonder who I might be able to help today with my contacts/knowledge?'

It really does make it easier when you are going into the situation with the agenda of helping others. Also, recognise that you are probably not the only person feeling anxious. Find other people looking as though they would rather be anywhere in the world than in that room at that moment, and engage them in conversation by asking them to talk about themselves. They will love you forever and you will instantly become the person they remember from that event – for all the right reasons.

Different questions

I'm sure you're aware of the 'open' and 'closed' questions.

Closed questions – invite a 'Yes' or 'No' answer and make it very difficult to maintain a conversation.

Open questions – cannot be answered with a 'Yes' or 'No' and can serve to open up the topic of conversation beyond the original question asked.

How you might start an open question conversation:

Who?

What?

How?

Where?

When?

Why?

Do be careful of the last one though 'Why?'. It can work very well, but if the context is slightly wrong and the tone of voice isn't just right, it may appear to be a little judgemental, so use wisely.

What do you do?

What is your most important project at the moment?

How did you get started in your business/job/profession?

Who do you know here?

Where do most of your clients come from?

How are you finding the economic climate at the moment?

When did you start your own business/profession?

How do you find the time to do all that?

What do you enjoy most about what you do?

Try and find a common discussion point – create rapport and start to build a bond. It's no mystery that a lot of men love to talk about sport (and some women for that matter). It's a really easy way to create that rapport and build a bond with someone, celebrating a team's win, commiserating about the thrashing at the weekend etc. It instils in people a sense of belonging, being part of the same 'tribe', an invisible thread of connection to other people that gives us our foundation and roots. So if you can establish a joint interest/hobby/love early on in the conversation it makes building that rapport so much easier and the relationship more sustainable.

For women, finding this common connection could be the trials of the working mother and the constant juggling, or the challenges faced operating in a male environment, or possibly similar leisure interests, to name but a few.

One of my examples:

I attended a Business Breakfast Networking group in March 2010 as the Guest Speaker. Over coffee, before we all sat down to eat, I got chatting to a lovely woman, I started the conversation by complimenting her on the wonderful colours she was wearing, as I was so used to entering a room full of black and grey!

She then told me she had been to India on holiday and was inspired by the use of colour and how happy it made her feel. I then told her I was going to India that April to do some work for a charity in Delhi. She had been to Delhi and told me all about it. We chatted for ages about this, at some point eventually getting round to discovering we were in similar fields with our businesses.

We kept in touch, I ran a weekend workshop for women with her company. As a result of that I had a phone call from someone who was organising an event for women in business who had been let down by their Guest Speaker. She had seen the leaflet about the workshop, and asked could I step in as the Guest Speaker and talk about my book?

If you build the right relationships, based on rapport and collaboration and genuine interest, you have absolutely no idea where they might lead you.

Your business or profession is based on your most recent conversation, people will remember the fabulous thing you did yesterday that impacted them, not what you achieved three years ago that you kept quiet about, hoping that people would find out by default. Trust me, they won't.

Why network at all?

Have you heard the phrase 'Six Degrees of Separation'? This means we all know at least 200 people, so you are never more than a few contacts away from the people you want to meet/talk to. With the phenomena that is social networking, the six degrees have decreased considerably, it's probably only about three now.

A few tips

Research who's going to be there

Try Googling the people you know are going to be at the event. Or find them via social networking. The more information you can have about attendees the better, as this creates an easy 'in' when trying to engage people in a conversation.

Set the outcome:

What is it you want to achieve? Are there specific people you want to get in front of, speak to, ask the opinion of? Do you have particular points you would like to get across to this group of people about a certain issue.

Reframe negative thoughts:

If you don't believe the meeting/conference/network is valuable, no-one else will. If you don't believe what you have to offer/say/ contribute is valuable, no-one else will.

Raising Your Profile

This can be done face-to-face, via your output and virtually

Face-to-face: Networking – Meetings – Public-Speaking Engagements etc.

Your output: Blogs – Articles – Books – Policy Papers – Guidelines etc.

Virtually: Facebook – Linked In – Ecademy – Twitter – You Tube etc.

Raising your profile is all about making sure people know you exist, ensuring you have a presence within your chosen industry/field/ area of expertise. Make sure *you* are the first person people think of, become the Oprah Winfrey of your sector!

How do you do that?

Well, first you need a Perfect Pitch.

If you don't know what you do, why you do it and why people should listen to you, you can guarantee no-one else will know either.

There is a tried and tested architecture to the perfect pitch:

Clarity	What is it that you do?
Credibility	Why should I listen to you?
Relevance	What's the problem that you have identified?

| **Believability** | What's your solution to that problem? |
| **Enthusiasm** | What's your 'mission', what are you known for? |

My Perfect Pitch

Clarity

I help women who work in male-dominated environments to have a strong voice, project themselves with authority and keep their femininity.

Credibility

I am a qualified executive coach, self-development trainer and personal-branding consultant. Since 1989 I have supported thousands of women with their careers. I have worked with many banks in the City. Most recently I have worked with over 180 policewomen from Constable to Chief Superintendant level on their communication and leadership skills. I have written articles for publications and appeared many times on BBC Radio.

Relevance

Over the years it has been evident to me that women are far more likely to beat themselves up rather than pat themselves on the back. This results in women being reluctant to push themselves forward in their career at the same rate as men. For organisations this can mean they have an out-of-balance management and leadership profile, which becomes more evident the further up the scale you go.

Believability

So I have developed a range of solutions, from one-to-one consultations where I can turn a woman round in two days, to group work from a one-day course to a five-day in-depth women into leadership programme run over three months.

I also have a book *The High-heeled Leader*, where women can work through the issues for themselves, in their own time, together with CDs and Blogs, keeping clients up-to-date with activities.

Mission

I am known for my energy and enthusiasm, together with my rock-solid belief in the absolute magnificence of everyone I work with.

My mission is to leave organisations feeling that they are doing something positive for women and making a difference, and to leave the women I work with feeling liberated, powerful, really excited about their future and ready to dance with life!

This pitch can be adapted for any situation – online profiles, twenty second emergency pitch for when you bump into just the person you've wanted to speak to while waiting for the lift, as the basis for a presentation from ten minutes to an hour, on your website, to create followers on Twitter – the list is, frankly, endless.

Have a go at creating your own Perfect Pitch

Clarity

....

....

....

....

....

....

....

Credibility

....

....

....

....

....

....

Relevance

....

....

....

....

....

....

Believability

....

....

....

....

Mission

....

....

....

....

If you want to learn more about creating your perfect pitch, I can highly recommend two books:

Become A Key Person Of Influence – Daniel Priestley

Find Your Light Bulb – Mike Harris

How we search for people nowadays has changed dramatically. The advent of social media has created a potential global market for everyone at the click of a mouse.

People expect to see more of you. Are you on/do you have:

Website

Facebook

Ecademy

LinkedIn

Twitter

You Tube

Podcast

Videos

Testimonials

Blogs

You don't have to run your own business to have this level of exposure. You have a lot to say whatever you do and wherever you do it.

How do you currently raise your profile?

....

....

....

What could you do better?

....

....

Be very aware, however, that anything on the internet is there for life. Make sure whatever content you enter and publicise is truly what you want everyone else to see, it may come back to haunt you if you get it wrong. We've all heard about the horror stories of pictures put on the internet from someone's past. It's very difficult to defend yourself when the evidence is out there for all to see.

Raising your profile face-to-face

Who within your organisation/in your business community needs to know about you?

How can you do it?

Can you volunteer for anything?

Can you put yourself forward for a particular project?

Can you sponsor a business event?

Can you get yourself on a Speaking Circulation list?

One of my examples:

When I was working in the City, the bank I was working with had something called The Staff Council. This was a body of thirteen people from across all areas and levels who represented all staff and presented their issues to Senior Management. I volunteered to represent my level. We met weekly and once a month presented any points for discussion to the Executive Committee – The President and Board.

Did I get paid extra for this? No. Did it raise my profile within the bank? Absolutely!

The bank had over 2,000 employees, yet if the President and I got in the lift together I was always greeted with 'Bonjour Katie, ça va?' He was French by the way, not trying to be smooth!

Whilst there I also organised a variety of lunchtime presentations by outside people on all sorts of subjects: meditation, breast cancer, prostate cancer, hypnotherapy, feng shui. These subjects had nothing whatsoever to do with the bank, but were of huge interest to the people who worked there. I used to regularly fill the auditorium with people.

One of the issues raised with The Staff Council regarded women bankers and their advancement at appraisal time. I presented this to the HR Director, who tasked me with setting up and heading a Gender Diversity Task Group, which I did. The members of that group were all considerably more senior to me at the time, but I was leading them.

I didn't get paid any extra in terms of cash for any of these activities, but the pay back was *huge*.

What do you think happened to my profile, visibility and credibility within the bank?

It went through the roof.

This level of visibility led me to my next role outside of the bank, where I worked one-to-one with leaders of FTSE 250 companies and networked with the movers and shakers, which resulted in me setting up my own company. The rest, as they say, is history.

THE PEACOCK OR THE OWL - WHICH ONE ARE YOU?

Do you hide in the background and hope no-one will notice you too much but automatically appreciate everything you do?

Or are you happy to shake out your feathers and be proud of your place in the world, confident that your presence has a beneficial impact on those around you?

What can *you* do in the next day, week, month to Raise Your Profile and ensure that the right people really know how amazing you are?

....

....

....

....

....

....

....

....

....

....

Why should you do these activities? What's in it for you and other people?

....

....

....

....

....

....

....

....

So, we've spent the last couple of chapters exploring ways in which you can have a strong voice with authority and impact. All this is fabulous and I know you will really see a difference once you get yourself out there in the world and are the wonderful charismatic woman I know you are. However, we can come up against all sorts of obstacles, one of them is the difference with how men and women communicate. A potential for conflict and misunderstanding the world over. So in the next chapter I will take you through some of the potential mistakes and give tips to overcome them in order to create harmonious communications with everyone.

Chapter Twelve
How Men And Women Communicate

'Because man and woman are the complement of one another, we need woman's thought in national affairs to make a safe and stable government.'
Elizabeth Cady Stanton

Did you know that men and women communicate in a completely different way and we are, in fact, two totally different animals? Who knew!

It's amazing how many people go through life getting really frustrated and confused because men don't think and speak like women and women don't think and speak like men.

Let's take a look at the basic differences. Then you can decide how much of the information about the differences is useful for you.

Millions of years of evolution is responsible for the 'stereotyping' we are all aware of between men and women, these character traits were there for a reason and will not disappear overnight.

Men

Their skin is much better at adapting to the cold (which is why you're wearing the bed socks and he's throwing the duvet off.)

Their bodies are usually leaner (damn them) and fitter.

Their eyesight is far more streamlined than women's – men are able to block out their peripheral vision far more effectively than we are.

Men's control hormone of testosterone enables them to excel at:

Map reading.

Hitting a target – except in the bathroom!

Playing computer games.

Having an inbuilt compass.

Parallel parking.

When faced with challenges they will:

Go back into the cave to think things over.

Only come out when they're ready.

Women

Our skin is much softer.

Our bodies are designed for endurance rather than short bursts of extreme activity.

Our eyesight is all encompassing and peripheral – yes we really *can* see out of the back of our heads.

Women are far more likely to negotiate or walk away in conflict situations.

Women think out loud and therefore seem to talk more.

Women are less direct in conversations and drop more hints.

Women multi-task more easily.

OK, I know these are generalisations and you will recognise stuff in the men's list that you do really well. I know I can parallel park a car brilliantly and am really good at reading maps – turning the map upside down in the direction of travel is just logical and good sense.

185

Now let's look at some of the above and think how that translates into the business arena.

Entering a room.

We will naturally scan looking for friendly faces and who we can build a relationship with. This makes us naturally good at networking as we enter the room with a completely different energy to men (who are likely to look for enemies first, friends second).

Hearing.

Because we naturally hear better than men, we are far more able to pick up the nuances of conversations going on around us, whether that's in a crowd of people, or just in the office. Very little will get past us.

Our ability to read body language.

Because we are more likely to pick up face-to-face lying, we make very good managers and leaders of people. It is hard, verging on the impossible, to pull the wool over our eyes.

Being able to detect atmospheres and understand how people are feeling, ensures we are naturally competent in the new, increasingly vital, leadership style of coaching and empowering.

How does this impact on our day-to-day conversations?

The potential downside of our natural skills, is that we assume absolutely *everyone* has them. We expect men to pick up on hints, and it comes as a bit of a shock when it clearly hasn't worked. Go on, you know you were cheesed-off when you received the new steam iron with matching ironing board last Christmas, surely he knew when you said 'something practical' what you *really* meant was a weekend in a luxury spa! After all, that is practical, if you feel better you operate better. But men really don't pick up on hints. They're not being difficult, honestly, they just don't have that ability. What they need are clear instructions, preferably with deadlines.

But if they just get hints, they can't work out what they're supposed to be doing. They may go into panic-mode which could kick in the testosterone aggression. They might then 'kick out' at us and pass the blame.

All this is avoidable if we simply give them clear instructions.

This is not about criticism or blame. It is about celebrating difference. If we can understand and respect differences, then all relationships will improve, everyone will feel better and harmony is maintained.

When it comes to face-to-face contact with men, we operate differently here too. As mentioned above, women use physical contact in conversation far more than men do, we touch people on the arm, the back of the hand etc. when we are building rapport. Some men can feel very uncomfortable with this, and may assume something completely different to the message you think you are giving. Just something to be aware of and think about.

When we are standing, we do that differently as well. Women are, generally speaking, quite happy to stand face-to-face with someone when in conversation. Men, generally speaking, are not. If you watch men in conversation they are far more likely to stand at slight right angles to each other, face-to-face indicates confrontation and potential aggression – they are getting ready to 'lock horns'. So if you are talking to a man and you are facing him head on, and he moves slightly, respect that otherwise you may find yourself doing a dance in circles as you each try and establish your positions!

How we both listen

The differences also extend to how we listen and absorb messages from other people.

If you find yourself in a meeting as the only woman, watch and observe what happens.

Most of the time men will remain completely static whilst listening, they don't make any listening 'noises', they don't move their bodies or their heads, their facial expressions tend to remain fixed. In other words they give nothing away, they won't 'show their hand' until they're ready. No coincidence that there are far more male poker players in the world than female.

Men are also likely to have an invisible ball (cricket/football/rugby/golf etc.) that they hold when they are speaking. The other men in the room will respectfully listen to whoever is holding the ball, the ball then gets thrown to another man, the rest turn and give that man their respectful attention.

Women listen *very* differently. We are keen to show our interest in what people are saying to us, so offer encouraging listening noises, 'Mmmm', 'Yes', 'I see', 'OK', 'Ah', etc. We move our bodies towards the speaker and incline our heads, implementing a whole range of facial expressions. We also nod repeatedly to show that we are listening and to give the speaker encouragement to continue.

So, men see this nodding, smiling, acquiescent woman in the room, assume she's agreeing with everything all of them are saying and don't bother to pass her the ball!

At the end of the meeting the men are summarising the agreed points, the woman in the room is feeling left out, irritated and ignored, and says, 'Excuse me, I have some points to make.'

The men look at her surprised and say, 'But you've been nodding and agreeing with us all morning.'

'No,' she says, 'I've just been listening.'

This has the potential to create confusion all round.

If you find yourself in a meeting or situation dominated by men and you need to make your point, be aware of the assumptions they may be making and try to mirror them a little more. This is not going against being true to who you are as a woman, it's simply to make your life easier, the situation less stressful and frustrating for you, and for you to get what you need and feel good. It's about getting the balance between being completely static and employing all the listening 'additions' we do without even being aware of them. If I find myself in this situation I don't mirror the men completely, but I do reign in the amount of movement in my body and face, I find it really difficult to speak without using my hands, so I try to have my hands occupied, making notes etc which makes it easier to keep still.

We talk as we're thinking, men process internally and only speak when they know what they're going to say.

So when you're speaking to your clients/colleague/partner/boss/ team member who's male and he's sitting there not moving, not looking at you and not reacting in anyway whatsoever, rather than getting angry and thinking to yourself 'He's not listening to a word I'm saying.' Remember he is, he just listens differently to the way you do.

Impact in the business arena

The opportunity for misunderstanding and potential conflict is potentially huge. As I've said earlier, we are different beings, we both bring great benefits to the workplace, it is just about being able to understand each other better to minimise the stress and maximise the harmony.

Women naturally tend to be more nurturing and better at face-to-face communication. Therefore some women may have a tendency to 'rescue'. Particularly if their dominant brain preference is limbic right.

I know this is true for me. What I've come to realise over the years is, actually, no-one wants to be rescued, particularly men. They haven't asked me to do it, and it's wrong of me to assume that's want they want. So I've stopped.

Men just want to reach the solution. Full stop.

If we go to men with an issue (you know what I'm going to say next), they will try and 'fix' it for us, and immediately come up with a list of solutions and then get very grumpy with us when we don't implement them. Actually all we wanted was for someone to listen to us off-load and give us a bit of empathy.

Trust me, this is unlikely to ever happen. Accept it, know it, and move on.

If you want empathy and a listening ear, go to another woman, whether that's at home or in the workplace, but particularly in the workplace. If you want a list of solutions, go to a man – give him instructions and let him do what he does best.

Body-language

Despite the differences in areas of male/female communication, there are some common body-language signals that we all use and it's helpful to be aware of what these are, the impact they may have and what it's good to try and avoid.

Always be aware of your posture – it can communicate a number of things:

Your posture can convey a whole range of attitudes, from interest or the lack of it, to degrees of respect.

When someone speaks they often use posture to punctuate what they are saying, shifting forward in their seat or leaning in towards the other person to emphasise an important point, or slumping back to indicate that they have finished making a point.

Eye-contact can have a very significant influence when you are inter-acting with other people:

It can play a key role in helping to establish rapport, failing to make eye-contact in many cultures is associated with being dishonest or having something to hide. Eye-contact also plays an important role in turn taking during conversation. Among a group of people, a speaker will often make-eye contact with the person he or she wants a response from. Someone who wants to enter or interject in a con-versation will catch the eye of the person speaking to indicate that they want to interrupt, and equally someone who no longer wants to listen will avoid eye-contact.

People who know each other well can communicate mutual under-standing with a single look.

Facial expression is one of the most obvious and flexible forms of communication and can easily convey mood, attitude, understand-ing, confusion and a whole range of other things.

Be aware of proximity, it is a far less obvious form of body-language but can be equally as meaningful. It is also something that can easily be misinterpreted as it can vary so much from culture to culture.

Open and closed body position – with open positions consisting of legs stretched out, elbows away from the body, hands not touching, legs uncrossed etc, and closed positions consisting of legs crossed at either knee or ankles, hands folded on lap, arms crossed etc.

People with open body positions are perceived more positively than those with closed body positions – no surprise there really.

People with open body positions are more persuasive than those with closed body positions.

Gesture can be used to replace verbal communication

Good public speakers will use hand gestures to illustrate what they are saying. It can also form part of punctuation with head nods and hand movements, which relate to the stress, rhythm and tempo of their sentences. Speakers who use their hands a lot often let them drop at the end of a sentence. Heads often nod down when words in sentences are stressed.

Congruence. Non-verbal signals have considerably more impact over verbal signals. If your verbal message happens to be 'Yes' and the non-verbal signals are saying 'No', which one are people going to believe?

Common Gesture Meanings

Gesture	When in moderate form	When exagerated
Forward lean	Friendly feelings	Hostile feelings
Direct eye-contact	Friendly feelings	Hostile feelings
Unique dress and hairstyle	Creativity	Rebelliousness
Upright posture	Expertise, self-confidence	Uprightness, hostility
Variability in voice pitch, rate & loudness	Lively mind	Nervousness, anxiety, insecurity
Smiling	Friendliness, relaxed and secure composure	Masking hostility, submissiveness
Averting gaze	Shyness, modesty	Guilt, unreliability
Knitted brow	Involvement	Hostility
Nodding and reaching out the hands while talking	Self-confidence	Uncertainty

Non verbal gestures to avoid	Common interpretations
Hair twirling	Incompetence and uncertainty
Placing your hand in front of your mouth	Anxiety about your competence
Rubbing your arm or leg	Anxiety about your competence, uncertainty
Wringing your hands, rubbing your fingers	Nervousness, anxiety, uncertainty
Slumped posture	Boredom, alienation

Transferring this into your working day

First off, don't lose your authenticity as a woman. We do operate differently to men. Whilst it's good to meet them halfway sometimes, it is never going to be good strategy to mirror them completely and become a clone of men in authority.

We do things differently, not better or worse, just differently. Appreciate and respect the differences, know when to approach men and with what, and when to go to another woman. Don't expect men to mirror us, they won't – ever. They simply don't have the capacity. They are not being difficult. Men are just not able to make the communication shifts that we can do in our sleep, so don't beat them up for it.

Finally, NEVER feel bad about your feminine communication traits, they are what make us unique, powerful and give us our authority. Be proud of them, use them to the very best of your ability and never compromise who you are to make other people feel more comfortable.

Just ease up on rescuing and try not to nod too much!

We're coming to the end of the book now, not quite, but getting close. Let's have a look at how you can embrace your feminine power in every are of your life, but particularly at work.

Chapter Thirteen
The Power Of
The Feminine At Work

'I would rather trust a woman's instinct than a man's reason.'
Stanley Baldwin

We have all experienced good and bad managers and business people in our time, regardless of gender. There are some fundamental behaviours that are crucial to good business practice. It is the responsibility of the person concerned to undertake these behaviours, to constantly assess their own performance against the criteria and take ownership of their own 'journey'. Not many people take the time or have the moral courage to do so.

Women are well placed in the world to take this responsibility. Our capacity for longevity of performance, emotional stamina and moral courage is huge. If women make themselves accountable at every stage of their journey they will automatically emerge as a force to be reckoned with and a benchmark of excellence for others to emulate.

Examples of negative business behaviour

No EQ (emotional quotient)

No political awareness (small 'p')

Problem focused

Delegate upwards

Focused on skill rather than people

Naïve about networks

Recruits weak replicas because they are threatened by talent

Bad delegators

Operates from comfort zone of authority rather than responsibility

Will manage a legacy rather than having the courage to make changes

Tries to be everyone's friend

Will abuse their status

Examples of positive business behaviour

Supports other people

Builds good, solid networks

Instils commitment and is a good influencer

Motivates everyone

Is self-aware and adaptable

Finds solutions not problems and will volunteer

Not averse to conflict and will manage it well

Communicates a clear vision

Has a 'can do' attitude

Excellent crisis-management skills

Decisive

Operates with honesty and integrity and is a role-model for others

Where are you on the previous pages? Tick every one that currently applies and capture where you could make improvements here:

....

....

....

....

The impact of the above on the organisation as a whole and the people within it is vast.

When the negative business skills are prevalent internally it is far more likely that a culture of mistrust, stress, uncertainty, resentment and competitiveness exists.

When positive business skills are the dominant style, conversely it is far more likely that a culture of trust, collaboration, sustainability, loyalty, collective vision and sharing exists.

Where would you prefer to work? Which business would you prefer to own and run?

If you are currently in the former and are not, at the moment, at the top rung of management, you may be sitting there thinking, 'I'm too small to be able to make an impact, change the culture or have a say'.

I'd like to quote the wonderful Anita Roddick who said

'If you think you're too small to have an impact on the world, try going to bed with a mosquito in the room.'

There are specific attributes in people that mark them out as having potential to manage people or run their own business:

Adaptability

Are you able to adapt to change in the organisation/business climate?

Are you able to adapt your management style to suit your team/clients? (think back to the chapter on How You Think)

Self-confidence

How much confidence do you have in your ability to do your job?

How much confidence do you have in your ability to manage people effectively?

How much confidence do you have to move up the career-ladder or to progress your own business?

How much confidence do other people have in you?

Being pro-active

How do you deal with challenges and crises?

With staff/client issues, how pro-active are you?

How do you plan for the future of your business?

How do you plan for the future of the organisation and your role within it?

Being reliable

Can people rely on you to be effective?

Can you be relied upon to be consistent with your style?

Ambition

How strong is your personal ambition?

How resilient is your ambition for the people who work for you?

How committed are you to the ambitions of the organisation you work for or the company you run?

Some of the above may cause some inner conflict. Ambition for example. If the ambition of the organisation results in tough decisions being made for some of the staff, and that has an impact on your team, you are likely to find yourself stuck between a rock and a hard place.

The good, effective manager will remain true to their values and beliefs, be clear about the vision, loyal to both the organisation and their team, and communicate messages with clarity, integrity, honesty and compassion.

The bad, ineffective manager will either 'side' with their team and bad-mouth the organisation, trying to remove themselves from the decision-making, or ruthlessly follow the vision without care or concern for those underneath them, as they see the changes being of personal benefit.

Go back to the above attributes and score yourself against each criteria one to ten, one representing poor performance, ten representing excellent performance.

Good business skills

Good business skills are a combination of many attributes, virtues, skills, personality traits and communication expertise. Whenever I ask groups I work with, 'What makes a good manager/business owner?' the same words always appear:

Enthusiasm

For the team; the people in the organisation; their company; their role; the role of others; new ideas; the vision; and 'can do' attitudes.

Integrity

A grounded, moral mind set; setting and sticking to a code of conduct; being clear of their values and living them; trustworthy and honest; completely incapable of being corrupt.

Warmth

Having a genuine and sincere interest in the welfare of others; being approachable and open; allowing mistakes through learning; empowering others to succeed and grow.

Courage

The ability to tackle any crisis with determination; moral firmness; vision; take appropriate risks; and create a feeling of protection and safety within others.

Judgement

Making appropriate decisions, however hard; solving problems head-on rather than delegating and hiding behind their authority; being good judges of character and seeing the best in others.

Tough but fair

Showing gentleness and compassion without being 'soft'; having a realistic vision of themselves and other people; showing strength and firmness but able to adapt and be flexible; being balanced with their treatment of people.

Let's face it, this isn't just how we work, this is how we live. We do all of this in our sleep, unconsciously, without even having to think about it. These are the values by which women live their lives.

We are born leaders, we do it every day, in every situation, naturally, easily, without thought or planning. Believe it, own it, and transfer that 'knowing' into the workplace.

The following I have adapted from the Domestic Abuse Intervention Project. You may be thinking this is a bizarre point of reference for this book, but when I was reading through the guidelines for good and bad behaviour and expected treatment of 'self', the correlations into good and bad business practice shouted out to me. See if you agree.

Power and Control – Violence

Using intimidation – making people afraid by using looks, actions and gestures.

Using emotional abuse – putting people down, making people feel bad about themselves, calling people names, making people think they are crazy, playing mind games, humiliation and instilling guilt.

Using isolation – controlling people's actions, their involvement in projects, limiting their access to information.

Minimising, denying and blaming – shifting responsibility for their actions, putting the blame on the person concerned, making light of complaints and not taking people's concerns seriously.

Using coercion and threats – involving people below them in their bad behaviour with threats if they don't get involved, threatening to not involve people in projects/give them a bad appraisal/overlook them for promotion etc.

I found it very sobering to recognise the similarities and also how aware I was that this kind of management and leadership behaviour exists.

The alternative, also adapted from the same project is:

Equality – Non Violence

Non-threatening behaviour – talking and acting in a way that people feel safe and comfortable expressing themselves.

Respect – listening to people non-judgementally, valuing the opinions of others, being emotionally affirming and understanding.

Trust and support – supporting the goals of others, trusting others' ability to do the job.

Honesty and accountability – accepting responsibility for self, being able to admit when they are wrong, communicating openly and truthfully.

Negotiation and fairness – seeking mutually satisfying resolutions to conflict, accepting change, being willing to compromise.

Let's explore this further in the context of behaviour within the workplace.

ASSERTIVENESS

> *'No-one can make you feel inferior without your consent.'*
> *Eleanor Roosevelt*

Assertive behaviour is at the very foundation of good management. It is also an absolute essential for all of us in how we live our lives. The most difficult person to be assertive with is yourself. Think back to your internal iPod. Most people are either aggressive or passive when they talk to themselves, usually aggressive.

'I don't believe it, I'm going to be late AGAIN, what an idiot.'

'I knew I should have taken that jacket in to be cleaned, now I've got nothing to wear!'

'Oh for ****'s sake, I've made the same mistake, when will I learn?'

'Will I ever learn this/get it right/be successful?'

So, before you try and be assertive with others, make sure you are treating yourself appropriately. It then becomes much easier to translate that out to the wider audience of other people.

Assertiveness and Confidence

There is a strong and direct link between someone's level of assertiveness and their confidence levels. The more naturally confident a person is, the higher their assertiveness, the less confident someone is, the more likely they are to demonstrate passive and/or aggressive behaviour.

Because most people do not allow themselves to make mistakes, they will try to cover up any feelings of inadequacy by going to one of the two extremes, either they will move into passive behaviour and hope no-one notices them, or they 'bluff' their way through situations with aggression.

Assertive people know that everyone makes mistakes sometimes, even them. They treat themselves and others kindly and with compassion when those mistakes occur, knowing it is a vital part of learning and life.

Assertive people work on the eighty/twenty rule. If they get their life right eighty per cent of the time, that's great, if they get it wrong twenty per cent of the time, that's great too. Striving for one hundred per cent all the time is both unrealistic and exhausting. It creates inner stress and outer conflict, it can alienate other people and isolate the perpetrator.

I intend to go to the gym five times a week, I usually make it around three – I can live with that.

I intend to eat really well and healthily every single day, I manage it about four to five days a week – I can live with that too.

How does behaviour impact on confidence levels?

Aggression – Confidence

People may be overly demanding on themselves and their capabilities.

They are likely to say 'Yes' to everything, believing that they can achieve whatever they set their mind to.

They don't take full advantage of making mistakes as a valuable learning tool.

They run the risk letting people down.

Passive – Confidence

People live with a 'can't do' mind set.

The To-Do list remains intact.

They feel powerless to act and react as they would like.

They operate with the 'not good enough' internal message.

They are always waiting to get 'found out' by others, even when they are successful.

They don't even bother trying.

Assertiveness – Confidence

People start things with a realistic and grounded mind-set.

They just get on with it.

Whatever the outcome, their self-esteem remains un-dented.

The outcome does not have to be guaranteed in order for them to try.

There is another behaviour that has always been very prevalent in business. Passive Aggressive. The office bully, the person who will put others down and make them feel small, ignore you when you're trying to speak to them, make snide remarks if you achieve something good etc. A really horrid behaviour style and very difficult to manage.

With all of the behaviour styles of Aggressive, Passive and Passive Aggressive, the important thing to remember is this. It is telling you how that person is feeling about themselves, *not* how they feeling about you. I've mentioned this in a previous chapter, but it's worth saying it again.

We all know that the playground bully was the biggest coward. Rather than waiting to get bullied themselves, they hit out first to create a wall of protection because they were feeling threatened. They were threatened by their lack of self-belief and confidence.

Unfortunately some of those playground bullies never learn and continue that behaviour into adulthood.

But if you can stand firm and secure in your assertive centre it makes it a lot easier to deal with them.

You may think that passive behaviour is OK, a bit sad, but OK. To be honest, it isn't. It can be as aggressive as overtly aggressive behaviour. I know that may not make sense, but the feelings it can manifest in other people can be extreme.

Have you ever been with someone who starts every sentence with 'Sorry...'? I want to reply 'Why, what have you done?'. People who will not look at you, who have a quiet voice and won't make any decisions, convinced they are rubbish at everything, are quite needy and want constant reassurance.

Be honest, what's your immediate reaction? It can be irritating to be around passive people and their behaviour is just as inappropriate and rude as aggressive behaviour.

'There is nothing enlightened about shrinking so others won't feel insecure around you.'

But all of these behaviours have the same underlying emotion, which is **fear.**

If you can recognise and acknowledge what is going on for someone internally, by not taking their behaviour personally, you are better placed than them in life. You are more likely to achieve, you are a magnet for others and are able to remain firm and balanced in your assertive centre.

I know this is hard, especially when you are face-to-face with inappropriate behaviour on a regular basis, it can be draining (if we allow it to be) and exhausting to deal with.

One of my biggest lessons in life, which I've already alluded to, is not to rescue everyone. I spent years thinking 'If they only did this, that and the other, they would be great/happy/successful etc'. The hardest life lesson for me has been to acknowledge, and accept, that some people are just happier being miserable! As this is so against how I live my life and my philosophy, this was incredibly difficult to take on board.

Knowing when to walk away from someone because, how ever much you believe in them, they are determined to never believe in themselves, is a very hard life lesson. There is only so much any of us can do to support and empower someone to be their best selves. Sometimes, it just isn't going to work, it may be part of that person's journey to have these experiences, and we don't have the right to get in their way and impose our joie de vivre on them. Hard – really, really hard. But occasionally essential.

So know which battles to fight. Know when you've been beaten and don't waste your valuable energy on people who want to stay exactly where they are. If you have to, and can, remove yourself from them, or remove them from you. Harsh lessons, but essential if you are to grow and become the shining light you were born to be. Don't let ANYONE get in your way, they don't have the right.

Part of being assertive with yourself is being personally aware of how you react to other people . I've already talked about the 'blame culture' that surrounds us. It is much easier to go through life passing the buck rather than having the courage to take responsibility.

I know you have that courage, otherwise you wouldn't be reading this book, and certainly wouldn't have got this far into it.

When I was younger and suffering from the malaise of uncertainty and lack of self-belief, I blamed everyone for everything, except myself. It was so much easier to hide behind the curtain of accusation rather than brush it aside and step onto the stage and accept my part gracefully.

Was I happy? Not even remotely. Did I face life with joy and a light heart? Hardly ever. Did I have great relationships? Dream on!

It wasn't until my early thirties I realised that if I kept having the same life experiences and was attracting the same type of person into my life, that perhaps it wasn't their fault. Maybe it had something to do with me. This was my 'light bulb' moment. It was then I started my own journey of self-discovery, accountability, responsibility and ownership of my life. I became my own leader.

It wasn't easy, far from it, it certainly wasn't pain free either, but boy, the joy and feeling of freedom at the end really made the pain worth every second.

Now if I meet someone for the first time and I find myself reacting negatively towards them – I may feel intimidated and not worthy or irritated and superior. Rather than instantly deciding I don't like that person and pushing the blame onto them for how I am feeling, I now take a step back and have a chat with myself. 'That's interesting,' I say, 'what button have they just pressed in me? What do I need to go away and look at again?'

Everyone we meet offers us a mirror. Whatever we need to look at within ourselves we will have reflected to us through someone else. So when you meet people who really hack you off, irritate you beyond belief, make you feel instantly angry, or you just want to curl up and disappear because the emotion of not being good enough is overwhelming – thank them.

They are there to offer you one of the greatest gifts possible. They are giving you an opportunity to learn about yourself, to heal on a deep level a past grief or issue, and enabling you to become even stronger, more powerful and full of joy.

If you ignore this message, the chances are you'll be given it again. What I've discovered is that the longer I ignore the message, the bigger the next message becomes. I've learnt to deal with the message and lesson when it is small and almost inconsequential, rather than hoping it will go away, only to be hit squarely between the eyes with a bat later on.

The great leaders of life are assertive. They don't blame. They take responsibility and ownership. They never stop learning – from themselves and other people. They are the shining light others want to follow.

Accepting that life is a continual gift and lesson is at the heart of the assertive person. Life is a joy and a celebration, and it becomes even more so if we take ownership of the part we play.

I just want to refer you back to the voice. If you are feeling nervous prior to a talk to a group of people, you may be feeling 'passive' inside, but your behaviour may appear 'aggressive' to the people looking at you. Let me explain.

You walk into the room and stand in front of a sea of faces. One person in the audience is smiling at you and giving you encouraging body-language. You're feeling a little apprehensive about your forthcoming talk so, when you start speaking, you focus your whole attention on the person who is friendly and smiling. What happens is that the person who is giving you encouragement begins to feel slightly uncomfortable with your intense focus on them and starts to have the internal thought 'I wish you would stop looking at me'. Everyone else in the room is feeling left out and ignored, and may become rebellious and feel the need to be disruptive.

Whatever happens, the chances are few people in the room will be listening *fully* to what you have to say.

So remember, however you are feeling internally, ensure you include everyone in the room with your eye-contact and attention. That way you will come across as confident and assertive.

Is it appropriate to be assertive in absolutely every situation? Probably not, no. This is about you living your life from an assertive mind set, and consciously moving to passive or aggressive if that is appropriate, rather than living passively and/or aggressively and consciously having to move to assertive.

What doesn't make sense, or is remotely realistic, is everyone living on a constant even keel of balance and equilibrium where no-one loses their temper, everyone is happy every minute of every day and peace and harmony prevail. This is real life, not a make-believe fairy tale.

Practise makes perfect, a boring old message from school, but true. No-one can go from passive to assertive overnight, or from aggressive to assertive overnight. It requires dedication to the cause, practice and commitment.

How much do you want it? Are you happy where you are or would you be happier moving to a more assertive centre? Think about the Action Planning with the Change Equation earlier. Is the joy of getting there greater than the pain of moving?

The more we practise the quicker that behaviour moves from being in our conscious competence to being in our unconscious competence – we just do it.

Let me explain in more detail what I mean by conscious and unconscious competence. Whenever we learn a new skill or mind-set, we all go through four stages:

unconscious incompetence - conscious incompetence - conscious competence - unconscious competence.

I know, a bit of a tongue and mind twister, I'll use the analogy of driving a car to explain.

When you were three or four years old, you couldn't drive, but you didn't know that you couldn't drive. At that age you thought this is how the world worked, you were always collected from point A and delivered to point B. You were *unconsciously incompetent* – you couldn't drive, but you didn't know that you couldn't drive.

Then you reach adolescence, you still can't drive, but now you *know* you can't drive. You're aware that this is a skill you can acquire when you're old enough. You are now *consciously incompetent*.

You get to the age when you can apply for your Provisional Driving Licence and you are now able to acquire the skills needed to drive a car. However, this isn't going to come easily – I can still remember my driving lessons: thumping headache, knotted stomach, sweaty palms and bum Super-glued to the drivers seat. I thought I was never going to get this. I can also remember my Driving Instructor saying 'Mirror, signal, manoeuvre', to which I thought 'At the same time? Are you mad!'. I was acquiring the skills, but I had to do everything consciously. When this happens you are in the state of conscious competence. You can do something, but you have to think about it.

Finally, you pass your test and you're out there driving. Some months later you are driving to work or doing a regular trip, you leave your home and arrive at your destination, you sit in your car and think to yourself "How did I get here?". You have no recollection of making the journey. You have now reached the point of unconscious competence. You just *do it*. Because you have practised the skills of driving repeatedly and consistently the process has made the transition to your unconscious mind, and that part of you takes over every time you get in the car. You are still able to react should something untoward happen while you're driving, but you are able to consciously think about other things, while your unconscious controls your hands and feet.

So don't despair if you feel you are never going to 'get' this assertiveness stuff. If you believe that assertiveness is not currently your default behaviour style, you are still three quarters of the way there. You are in the conscious competence stage, you can do it, you just have to think about it first. Know, though, that the more you practise, the quicker this assertive behaviour will make the transition into your unconscious and you *just do it*, without thinking, planning or stress.

Think about situations you find yourself in and judge for yourself how you currently behave, then think how you would like to behave. If it is helpful, write your thoughts beside each example.

At home with your partner

At home with children

At home with other family members

At work with managers

At work with team members

At work with clients

With friends

With strangers socially

With strangers when work related.

Other areas of your life – in shops/on holiday/doctor etc

Is there anything you need to do to move yourself from where you are now with your behaviour to where you would like to be?

Capture any thoughts here:

....

....

....

....

....

....

....

Let's look at other areas of performing well in life and business. I've already talked about what women on my programmes have said when asked the question 'What makes a good manager/business owner.' There are other dimensions to being effective in life and work. We'll take a look at these now.

MANAGING YOUR ENERGY

Minimising the lack

How do you manage your work/life balance?

How good are you at prioritising – both at work and at home?

How good are you at maintaining enthusiasm?

Topping up

How good are you at keeping your energy levels overflowing?

How good are you at keeping focused and not letting distractions take you off course?

Being in the 'flow'

Do you manage to be so engaged with projects that you are not aware of time – are you 'in time' or 'on time' focused?

When in flow, how do you maintain your energy levels and not allow yourself to become drained?

CAN-DO MIND SET

Being self-aware

Do you acknowledge your skills and talents regularly?

Do you give yourself a pat on the back when appropriate?

Staying positive

How well do you cope with change and challenges?

How much to you 'buy in' to the collective negativity of others?

Moving forward

Can you shake off negative experiences and not take them personally?

Do you pass the buck and blame, or take responsibility and ownership?

MAKING CONTACTS

Building networks

Do you have them? How good are you at it, internally and externally?

Empowerment of other people – how much do you help others to grow?

Win/win

It is all about what you get out of others, or do you understand and operate with a win/win mindset. Do you help other people succeed as your first priority?

Being inclusive

Are you able to see the people you work with as 'people' who bring the whole range of human emotions with them to the office?

Are you willing to ask for help when you need it?

BEING VISIBLE

Your voice

Do you manage to have a strong voice, especially when you are in a male-dominated arena?

How happy are you to accept praise and take credit where credit is due, allowing yourself to shine?

Ownership

How much do you own your journey of life?

Do you allow other people to dictate your progress?

Taking risk

Are you happy to accept that the status quo is not always possible and sometimes taking risks is part of your job?

How much do you retreat into the background for safety?

Flexibility

Do you always have the end goal in mind, and are you never prepared to go off track, ever?

Or are you prepared to explore other avenues, being open to the knowledge that you don't know everything?

LIFE PURPOSE

Being happy

I have a cover for my iPhone that says 'Life's too short not to love what you do.' How much do you love what you do?

Are you head or heart led? Are you willing to accept that sometimes your heart knows better?

Are you happy letting everyone else know how amazing you are?

Leaving your 'dent' in the universe

What impact do you want your time on earth to have?

How will people benefit from you being here, perhaps even after you've gone?

Think about yourself and all of the above. What are you currently honouring with how you live your life right now? Are there any areas you would like to address and improve on?

Capture your thoughts here:

....

....

....

....

....

....

....

....

....

....

....

I've mentioned earlier in this chapter that 'integrity' is a word that appears every time people think of good managers. But what does that mean exactly and how can you measure it? We would all say we live with integrity if asked, no-one would be willing to say otherwise. But is this something we can claim for ourselves, or is it a title only other people can bestow upon us?

How well do you inspire and motivate people to follow you and allow them to be the best they can be?

That is integrity – how other people are around you, how they instinctively react and behave

Do all women make great managers? Well, that depends on the woman of course. There are great and not so great examples of both genders. With both sexes, it is ultimately down to that person's courage and ability to take ownership of who they are, their level of self-belief, their lack of fear and compassion for others.

I have known men who are wonderful at all of the above, and some women who are not.

There is a misconception sometimes that all men are hard, ruthless and calculating and all women are nurturing and empowering of others. Not true. I've had some women on my courses who have had a nightmare of a female boss and an angel of a male boss.

BUT – with our natural characteristics and ability to be all seeing and flexible, if women absorb the attributes of good business skills and are willing to come out from behind the curtain, are willing to shout proudly about how good they are, are able to overcome their lack of self-belief and stop blaming everyone for their lack of progression, then we do make

FABULOUS, MAGNIFICENT AND AMAZING LEADERS
OF OTHER PEOPLE AND OF OUR OWN LIVES.

As women we can be seen as the willow tree. Willow trees, on first glance, appear to be fragile and less grounded or secure as the oak.

However, when there is a hurricane blowing, which tree is better equipped to cope? The willow. The fact that it is more flexible and pliable is at the centre of its innate strength and power.

The oak, on the other hand, by its very immovability and rigidity makes it more vulnerable at times of nature's challenges. This was hugely evident during the storms of late 1980s. Living proof that the solid oak is not, actually, as resilient or strong in times of crisis as its more flexible and 'feminine' willow cousin.

So never underestimate the power of the feminine, taken into the work and business environment, it gives us our inner core of power and strength, which not even a hurricane can topple.

You've now reached the end of Part Four, and are about to enter into creating the future you deserve and desire. This is the time to get really excited and start feeling the lightness and flutter of expectation in your heart. Really feel in your body the fizz of joy and happiness, now deep within every cell of you that you can create whatever future you dream of. Believe, dream, achieve.

'Twenty years from now you will be more disappointed by the things you didn't do than by the ones you did do. So throw off the bowlines. Sail away from the safe harbour. Catch the trade winds in your sails. Explore. Dream. Discover.'

Mark Twain

Part Five
Time For Celebration

Chapter Fourteen
Your Story

'Don't wait for a light to appear at the end of the tunnel.
Stride down there and light the bloody thing yourself.'
Sara Jane Henderson

This is the really exciting bit. There is very little that is more powerful and life-enhancing than taking the dreams out of your head and creating a tangible representation, something you can see, feel, touch.

It brings your dreams to life, gives them their own voice and personality, ignites your energy and passion, makes them REAL.

Before we start, have you congratulated yourself for getting this far? I think you should. Whatever turns you on, chocolate or champagne for example. But have what you love by your side and celebrate transforming your wonderful visions into a tangible reality.

YOUR MAJOR TURNING POINTS

What have been the major turning points of your life?

When have you gone through periods of extreme change?

Looking back, when have you lived through trauma, of any kind?

Where were the 'light bulb' moments – the times when you had a breakthrough in your thinking?

When did you come out of your comfort-zone and achieve something you didn't think you were capable of?

Capture these important milestones of your life here:

....

....

....

....

....

....

....

....

....

....

....

....

....

....

....

....

....

What did you learn about yourself during these times and experiences?

....

....

....

....

....

....

....

....

....

....

....

What are you really proud of?

....

....

....

....

....

....

....

....

....

....

Write a review of yourself

Imagine you are reviewing a biography of yourself and writing a recommendation. What would you write? Make sure you capture all your good points, including everything you have learnt along the way, and don't hold back.

....

....

....

....

....

....

....

....

LOOKING AFTER YOURSELF

You are your most precious asset. Make sure you celebrate that asset and look after it, nurture it, honour it and nourish it.

Mind – Body – Spirit

If we honour each of the above aspects of ourselves, we can't go far wrong in life. I know when I look after all these parts of 'me' I feel balanced, stress-free and full of optimism.

Mind

There are various ways in which you can look after your mind, which also fall into the category of body as well.

Exercise
Stick with me! I know the thought of the gym can be a bit like a nightmare come true, but I'm not talking about 'feeling the burn' or hours of training. If we exercise it releases endorphins, the 'feel good' hormone, this results in lifting our mood and giving us more energy and enthusiasm for life. A brisk, regular walk will do, taking the stairs instead of the lift, dancing.

Food
Some food will lift us and give energy, some will deplete us and make us feel tired, irritable, bloated. If you are not sure which foods work for you and which you may be intolerant to, I recommend you get yourself tested. It can make all the difference and take you from tired to alive in a few days. Some food groups are fabulous as 'brain food'. Fish oils are fabulous for our brains, so incorporating oily fish a few times a week will make us feel great, they are also good for memory and creating the neural pathways in our brain.

Meditation
I don't necessarily mean the lotus position every morning chanting before going to work. Although if that's what you do, that's wonderful. I mean allowing your mind to be still on a regular basis, shutting

down the conscious mind 'chatter' that can overstay its welcome, and letting your mind rest, regain its balance and serenity. A soak in a bath with candles and some restful meditation music will work magic. Listening to the same music on your journey to or from work will do too. I know I find it really difficult to meditate on my own, but find when I'm in a group that the discipline is incredibly powerful and I always feel better afterwards, so think about joining a group, or starting one.

Body

Exercise
Yep, we're back here again. But we are dictated to by our hormones, one of which is oestrogen, which depletes dramatically post menopause. This depletion is the main reason for osteoporosis, the horrid bone shrinking disease that can afflict us in later life and make breaking our bones more likely and far more serious. One way to help protect our bones is to do weight bearing exercise before the menopause kicks in, this type of exercise will help strengthen our bones while the oestrogen is still there in full supply. Another symptom of our sedentary lifestyles is stiff joints. Exercise and movement will help keep us supple, our muscles elongated and strong, which in turn help to support our skeleton and maintain our posture, now and as we age. Yoga (also great for the mind) and pilates are wonderful for suppleness and strength.

Spirit

Your attitude to life
How do you view the world and people in it? How do you view yourself? It has been proved that people who have a 'positive mental attitude' are generally much happier in life, suffer less depression, less illness and increased longevity, health and wellbeing.

Where do you live?
By that I mean are you focused on the past and previous pain, or the future and potential stress. Or are you focused on the present

226

moment? Yes, the past is important as it's had an impact on who we are today. But it's gone so don't dwell there and lose your energy to things you can't change. Yes, the future is important as it helps us set our goals and it's where our dreams lie, it's crucial to think and plan for our future, but don't let the future have the monopoly on all your thought forms. The present is actually all we have at any given moment. When the future arrives, it is the present. Remember to 'smell the roses' along the way. Be fully present with everything you do, live it NOW, relish the experience, feeling, emotion, texture, taste, touch and aroma.

Spirituality
Whatever your beliefs, living your life according to a particular mind set can be hugely beneficial. Whether that is a recognised religion, spiritual belief, or simply a 'way of being', knowing what you stand for in life and living accordingly will give people a sense of purpose. Make sure you know what your sense of purpose is.

However you cherish and nurture your most precious asset, please make sure you do, you are special, very special and you deserve the best of everything that can feed you.

YOUR VISION FOR THE FUTURE

To kick-start you thinking about your future vision, I want to tell you a story. It's a story of women living in a place called Stagnation Town, a business fairy tale.

Once upon a time there lived a group of women. Although they were all unique and special women, they had a lot in common. They were mostly working in male-dominated environments, running their own businesses, making their mark in companies and trying to leave their own dent in the universe.

Almost all of these women were happy when you described them as high-achievers, unique, fabulous, powerful and feminine.

Despite all the things that were good in Stagnation Town, some of these women were not one hundred per cent happy or satisfied with their life.

They were frustrated because there was way too much inner resistance to change, lack of self-belief and confusion. These women could also fall into the trap of blaming the companies they worked for and the general business culture, for their own lack of success.

There wasn't enough collaboration, trust and confidence. These women also wished there was more communication and respect generally. Ideally they would have preferred a little bit less: testosterone in the workplace, resistance from themselves, their own fear and living in a blame culture. Sadly they could get quite emotionally low thinking about how hard it all was and believed that they couldn't be themselves. Secretly they hated female 'ball breakers', and sometimes, sadly, themselves. It really hacked them off when they couldn't be authentic and their secret fear was they wouldn't be good enough and they needed to lose their femininity in order to gain power in the workplace.

Quite often these women would find themselves dreaming of a far away place where things were different. In this new place things were brilliant because they could be themselves and they were always respected. They felt really great about stepping into their power and being seen. They didn't have to worry about losing their essence and sense of self. They were proud of who they were and their place in the world. But, best of all, there was a top-secret rumour that in this far away place people would regularly get balance, happiness, joy and fulfilment. The women called this place Paradise City. Some of them had been there briefly and wanted to get back, some of them had never been there but it sounded amazing.

The problem was that when it came to Paradise City, they knew this place existed but they just couldn't get themselves there. They believed there were too many obstacles in their way.

For example, most of the women believed that in order to get there they would have to sacrifice part of themselves, their femininity, their very essence. They were also worried that people would alienate them and they would lose friends. They also feared that they wouldn't have enough time, energy, courage or ability to get there.

What they didn't understand was, that by honouring who they were will always be more powerful than trying to behave like the men. But their worst fear of all was a big monster that no-one spoke of, but everyone secretly feared. The monster was a mind reader and it would shout out people's worst fears and then paralyse them into indecision.

Of course the big secret fear that most of these women had was that they weren't really good enough and it was too 'pushy' to promote themselves and dare to dream.

However, some women were brave enough to take the Magic Pill of Self-Belief and Confidence and were amazed when they experienced fast-acting relief from the pain of doubt, struggle and lack of opportunities. They gained freedom from the frustration they had previously had when they didn't know how to 'be' or behave. And they said goodbye to their past regular headaches of how much of themselves to give. They realised that when they took the Magic Pill they were motivated to take responsibility and action and very quickly they started to become aware of the side-effects of joy, confidence, personal power, respect and clarity. They began to feel positive about their future and their ability to take risks.

There were, however, some treacherous mistakes along the way to Paradise City that some women unfortunately fell foul of. These were:

Not knowing their own power and magnificence.
Forgetting to ask for help and plan their future.
Thinking they will get promoted/win the deal on their skill alone.
Not having a great network or being sufficiently visible.

Thinking they had to behave like men.
Doing nothing – just staying where they were and complaining.
Not taking responsibility and not being accountable to themselves.

There was an oracle at Stagnation Town who had a crystal ball that could predict the future of women who fell foul of the treacherous mistakes, and didn't change what they were doing, or how they thought.

The crystal ball often predicted things such as:

If you stick with what you are doing, you will start to experience increased stress and disenchantment, continued blame and inner imbalance.

People who did what you are doing were disappointed that other women succeeded with ease.

If only you knew that your fate was to be paralysed, earn less, be frustrated and waste your abilities.

Change your ways or else you will likely be full of regret and die frustrated and angry.

Don't wait until other people do what you know you are brilliant at.

This oracle also used the crystal ball to predict what could happen if women moved past the treacherous mistakes and took risks. It predicted they could have:

A future of authenticity, joy, light, magnificence and wonder.

The ability to step into their power with absolute certainty.

The power to own their place in the world with pride.

The tools to help other women along the way and create a world full of energy, enthusiasm and collaboration.

The crystal ball's predictions were so compelling that more and more women joined the journey to Paradise City and the tipping point became so powerful that they changed the world.

The moral of this story is that it is imperative you tell your own story. Create your own vision of your future and then take action to ensure that vision becomes your reality. Be a part of the collective tipping point – you CAN change the world.

The person you were yesterday is dead. The person you are going to be tomorrow hasn't been born yet. Who do you want her to be?

Dreams V Goals

Dreams are those lovely, day dreaming, far away thoughts of what life would be like 'if only'. If you keep them in your subconscious day dreaming folder, that's all they will ever be – dreams.

But once you take them out of that folder and download them onto your hard drive, print them off and *see* them, they become part of your achievable reality.

What would you prefer – dreams or goals?

A lot of people are scared of setting goals. They believe that if they make something that 'real' it will be limiting, throw them into un-movable grid lines with no opportunity for movement. Actually the reality is completely different. Goals allow you far more flexibility and movement in your life than if you don't have them. If you have no idea of where you are going, you can guarantee that you will never get there.

Goals give you choices. They allow your mind to expand not con-tract, because dreams can appear so unrealistic that you are likely to reign yourself in, but once you see them in front of you, you actually realise you can aim a lot higher/further.

Reach for the edge of the Galaxy – if you miss, you'll still land amongst the stars.

Goals help you decide what you *really* want. Remember the chapter on clothes and budgeting? If you budget you can afford anything. If you set goals you can achieve anything.

And never forget, these are your goals, no-one else's. If you want to change them, go in a different direction, move the goal posts, you can. No-one has ownership of your goals except you.

Goals allow the power of your unconscious mind (which has all the answers) to have expression, goals transport that inner knowing you were born with to live, breathe and blossom.

I can take you through the Ten Steps to Successful Goal Setting, you can download this from my website.

Vision Boards

Ooh, now, these are fun. A real opportunity to play and let free your wonderful creativity. Remember, all of these are for your eyes only, you don't have to share with anyone if you don't want to.

Spend some time thinking about the area of your life you would like to concentrate on. Then buy yourself a large sheet of artist card, anything from A3 upwards. Get some glue and a pair of scissors and a whole stack of magazines, doesn't really matter what kind.

Then just randomly flick through the magazines without any pre-conceived ideas or judgement, and every time you see a phrase or image that resonates with you, cut it out. When you think you've got enough, lay them all out so you can see them all clearly and then decide which ones 'sing' to you and enhance your vision.

Then randomly (this is really important - don't be precise, neat, lin-ear or controlled) stick them onto the sheet.

Then sit back and smile! This is such a colourful, glorious and fun way to visualise your future. It stimulates the creative, right side of the brain and gives your unconscious permission to fire up and find ways of achieving for you what it's looking at. It helps to 'download' into your brain your future, transforming it from future impossible to present possible.

If your mind 'sees' your future as being 'now', it will assume it is already happening. You start to live 'as if' rather than 'I wish'. This opens up an avenue of opportunity for you. You suddenly become more awake to the possibilities out there, you begin to believe that you're there already and you will find opportunities coming at you from all angles, from where you least expect them, your life becomes truly synchronistic.

Get really excited by what you're looking at, believe and create your own possibilities.

Your Personal Agreement

This is an agreement between 'you' and 'you'. No-one else is involved.

Where do you want to be and who do you want to be?

Who are you in two years, three years, five years time? Choose a future time that works for you.

What are you doing? Who is in your life? How much are you earning? Where are you living? What personal development have you achieved? How at peace are you? How happy and joyful are you?

Now, write it down – be bold, be proud, be joyful.

Start in the present tense : 'I am ....' as though you are already there and everything is already happening.

Breathe it into every fibre of your body.

I am

....

....

....

....

....

....

....

....

....

....

....

....

....

....

....

....

....

....

....

....

....

....

....

....

....

....

....

Now read it back.

How do you feel? *Excited?* Do you want to be there?
Is anything going to stop you?

BE PROUD, VERY PROUD

YOU'VE ACHIEVED A HUGE AMOUNT IN
YOUR LIFE ALREADY AND YOU'VE
ONLY JUST BEGUN

GO OUT INTO THE WORLD AND SHINE
YOUR BRIGHT LIGHT OF MAGNIFICENCE

BE A BEACON FOR OTHERS TO FOLLOW

AND

DANCE
WITH LIFE

RESOURCES

If you would like to work with me, please take a look at my website for information on what I could deliver to support you and how to contact me

www.katieday.com

You can also find me on the following:

http://www.twitter.com/KatieDayAuthor
http://www.facebook.com/KatieDayConsulting
http://www.uk.linkedin.com/in/katiedayconsulting
http://www.ecademy.com/user/katieday3

Extra resources offered for your mind, body and spirit, all delivered by fabulous, magnificent women. I can highly recommend every single one of them.

Hypnotherapy for women.
Rosie Harness
www.harness-hypnotherapy.co.uk
rosie2harness@gmail.com

Bodytalk Therapist.
Angela Kirk
angela.wellhealed@gmail.com

Nutritionist.
Jude Price
www.judeprice.com

Natural Health & Wellbeing Consultant
Specialist in skin health, clearing blocks to healing and self-empowerment.
Elaine Copeland
www.elaine-copeland.com
enquiries@elaine-copeland.com

Emotional and practical mentoring to support you to let go of what doesn't work, grow what does and be all you are.
Caroline Sherrard
caroline@inspiredlearning.co.uk

Healing Energetics for mind and body.
Emily McMorran
Emilyjane39@gmail.com

Retreats

Lorrens Health Hyrdo
A women-only health spa in Torquay, Devon
A truly wonderful space, an absolute must for every woman
www.lorrens-health-hydro.co.uk
enquiries@lorrens-health-hydro.co.uk

Witherdens Hall, Canterbury, Kent
A beautiful, restful space and wonderful environment.
www.witherdenshall.co.uk
louise@witherdenshall.co.uk

Additional

Mindfulness at Work, find stillness in a busy world.
www.mindfulnessatwork.com

Invisible Goddess
Healing and transforming the lives of women coming through divorce and separation.
www.invisiblegoddess.com
Desiree@invisiblegoddess.com

If you run your own business and would like to take that business to the next level, then I strongly recommend the following programme:
Become A Key Person Of Influence.
Go to www.triumphantevents.co.uk to find out more.

Bibliography

Adair John, *The Inspirational Leader*, 2009

Mind Management Ltd, 2006

Mulvey Kate, Richards Melissa, *Decades of Beauty*, 1998

Owen Jo, *How To Lead*, 2005

Willis Liz, Daisley Jenny, *Springboard*, 2001

CPSIA information can be obtained at www.ICGtesting.com
Printed in the USA
LVOW042240260712

291550LV00003B/1/P